I Found Myself in Tuscany

Lisa Condie

Cover image David Newkirk david@davidnewkirk.com

Library of Congress Cataloging-in-Publication Data available upon request

Editorial work Connie Tucker and Caroline Larsen with Eschler Editing
Cover design: Rochelle Tolman
Interior print design and layout: The Printed Page
eBook design and layout by The Printed Page

First Edition: 2017
Printed in the United States of America
10 9 8 7 6 5 4 3 2 1
ISBN 978-0-692812129

For Justin and Lauren,
the only two who had a vote

Year One ~ 2012

We shall not cease from exploration, and the end of all our exploring will be to arrive where we started and know the place for the first time.

—T. S. Eliot

Prologue

My relationship with Italy has traveled much the same course as any new love affair. First there is infatuation, then the stark reality of imperfections, and, finally, a contented acceptance that binds us together.

Each phase took about a year, and I have finished all three phases now. The third phase of contented acceptance crept in slowly, almost unnoticed. I smile at how far I have traveled, because the change has, of course, been mine. Italy does not change.

This beautiful, enchanting country paints each new day with its glorious light, and initially, I saw what everyone sees. A slower-paced, charming lifestyle—the *dolce vita*! Italy was gorgeous fashion, fabulous food, and wine that flowed like water. So began year one.

However, living here for an extended period of time can be difficult: for everyone, but even more so for *stranieri*—strangers, like me. There is the bureaucracy that strangles its government; there are train strikes, rubble, and taxes, all bearing down on a country that seemingly has no capacity to respond. The cracks became evident in the façades as daily living in Italy became my reality. That was year two.

But here is the amazing part about Italy—it does respond! While buildings crumble and paint peels, while garbage piles higher, life goes on. Surrounded by pastels and drizzled with olive oil, life in Italy continues to go forward and prosper. And so did I.

My daily rituals, easily performed in my home country, were now performed here. The novelty of my new home wore off, but my acceptance of a different life ripened into deep affection. That was year three.

While I navigated through the days in my new country, it changed not one bit. For centuries Italy had seen starry-eyed women gravitate to its charms, and it bent not an iota. But I did. I bent in learning to understand a different culture, a new approach in how to live, a new rhythm to dance to, and a new language to speak.

Much like learning to drink its bitter-tasting espresso, Italy provides the challenge. It asks you to know it better, to dig in deeper, and it rewards those who are resilient enough to do so with an inexplicable joy that I have found nowhere else in the world. Its initial deception had been, of course, in convincing me it would be easy.

One

October 2012

My eyes were closed, but I was not asleep. I stretched my legs slightly and readjusted, yet again, the too-small piece of foam that was passing for my pillow. Inside the airplane was dark, and open-mouthed strangers were sleeping all around me. But I didn't sleep.

Somewhere over the Atlantic Ocean, my decision of a lifetime started to sink in. My throat felt tight, and the sensation was traveling down to my stomach. I was thirty-seven thousand feet in the air between what once was home and my new home in Florence, Italy. For the first time in three months, I was filled with apprehension.

I had sold or given away almost everything I owned, save a few possessions—more sentimental than valuable—that were now in a storage unit in Salt Lake City. I had two suitcases in the belly of the aircraft and a carry-on bag with my trusty electronics. I was traveling light but with almost everything I currently owned.

I'd either had too much or not enough wine with dinner, because sleep was elusive, and my thoughts were heavy.

Oh my God, what have I done?

Two

Three months earlier—June 2012

While I can't remember the exact day, I do remember I needed some coffee. It was six-fifteen a.m., and I was waiting outside my hotel in Rome for a taxi that would take me to the airport. My two-week dream vacation was over, and I was returning home to Salt Lake City. Two doors down was a coffee shop, not yet open, but the door was unlocked, and I asked if I could come in.

As I waited for my coffee, I breathed in the brewing espresso and the baking pastries. I listened to the lilt of Italian coming from the back kitchen.

And then, I started to cry. In that moment, I made a decision. The decision was that I would come back to Italy, and soon, but not on another vacation. I would come back to live in Italy, and whatever hold it had on me could fully run its course. I'd felt something there that I hadn't felt in a very long time: *joy!* And I wanted to feel more of it.

There was no logical reason for a middle-aged woman of Danish ancestry, born and raised in Utah, to think she belonged in Italy. There was no logical reason for me to sell my home, turn over my business, and leave my fitness students, lifelong friends, and family to start a new life—alone.

It had seemed to be my soul speaking, and with all my heart, in that instantaneous decision, it had seemed so right.

There was something in Italy that was drawing me back, almost as though I were going home, and it was the only place in the world I wanted to be.

The trip in 2012 had begun as a cruise out of Italy, to Greece and Turkey, then back to Rome. It was supposed to have been a wildly romantic birthday celebration for Thomas as a gift from me....

But as the date for the cruise drew closer, we drew further apart, until the last argument, which had left no doubt. We were no longer a couple.

The last-minute scrambling had my daughter joining me for the romantic cruise, and ultimately she was the first person I told about my decision.

As I stepped outside of that coffee bar in Rome, I watched the sun brilliantly streaming through the tall buildings and off the white marble of the opera house. My daughter had seen my tears as I sat down in the taxi beside her.

"You okay?" she said.

"Yeah, I am," I told her. "I'm coming back here. To live."

I'd looked straight ahead, not daring to see her reaction.

"I think you should, Mom. I've never seen you happier."

And there it was: I'd said it out loud, and confirmation was the first response. Yes!

Once the plane landed in Utah, the whirlwind of activity and decisions began. I gave myself three months to sell my home and possessions, wrap up my businesses, and say goodbye to Utah.

At least fifty times a day, I would walk by a mirror, stop and look myself in the eyes. "I'm going to Italy...to LIVE!" It charged me with energy and excitement each time, and I zipped through the blur of days and details.

It was at this point that I began to learn the first of many new life lessons.

Not everyone was going to be thrilled about my new adventure. Most were mildly surprised, fairly supportive, but some were downright dream-squashers. They pointed out things like I didn't speak Italian, and I didn't know a single person there.

They wanted to know where I would spend Thanksgiving, and what my children thought. And, of course, the recurring theme that I had, yet again, not been able to keep a relationship going with a man.

I did my best to push those thoughts away and concentrated on the job at hand.

There were a few people, however, who totally embraced my choice to go. I could see it in their eyes. Most of them older, most of them women. They knew.

They knew how small the window of time can be for us to act on a dream.

An old college friend sent me a bracelet with the inscription, *Woman of Courage*, and I put it on immediately. Was I a woman of courage? Was courage what was propelling this gigantic move across the ocean? I wasn't sure. Was I running to a new life, or running away from an old one?

I entertained those thoughts briefly but stayed connected to the tasks at hand. They were plentiful and demanding, and introspection had to be placed on hold.

I simply refused to entertain the notion that I couldn't sell my house, and most everything in it, quickly and easily. That was the intention I had placed in the Universe, as well as my heart, and that's the intention I was holding to. It just meant that on a daily basis, I had to let go of something else.

I had to surrender to a bigger picture. (May I just add that I am thirty-seven pairs of designer shoes lighter? *That* was painful.)

I learned, in those three months, valuable lessons—the biggest one, to just take the next step that seemed best for me. Most of those ninety days were a whirlwind of decisions. While some were big decisions, it was the sheer volume that had my head spinning. So many variables were unknown to me. How long would I need a storage unit? Where did I want my apartment to be in Italy? Who would teach my Pilates class? Was I going for three months or forever?

I began every morning with a calming meditation. While not always easy to calm down my monkey brain, I forced myself to be still for fifteen minutes each morning and listen to my breath. I believe it taught me how to make decisions with efficiency, trust my intuition, and visualize the end result.

If doors opened, plans presented themselves, and people appeared, I knew I was headed in the right direction. If it felt like I was pushing a boulder upstream, rather than going with the flow, I knew I had to change plans.

On October 2, 2012, I boarded Delta flight #89 to Florence, Italy, via Paris.

Behind me was a house that had sold and closed in six weeks, a storage unit, students who cheered me on, lifelong friends, and my son and daughter.

Ahead of me—unknown.

Three

I slid the flap on the airplane window up slightly and peered into the dark night sky. I tried to remember the feeling of Italy. I tried desperately not to lose the certainty that I was doing the right thing. I felt a little nauseated. What was it about Italy that had grabbed me that morning and begged me to come back?

I decided to leave the esoteric questions alone, as my brain was sluggish, and I settled on the practical. I had enrolled in a language school and would begin the first week of November. When I applied online, the school had contacted me regarding whether I wished to live with a family or in an apartment with five other girls.

I'd quickly fired off an email to the school's secretary informing her that I was a fifty-six-year-old woman and would need my own apartment. I'd asked for recommendations of landlords in Florence, since my dorm life days were clearly behind me.

The school had sent Lorenzo Clemente's contact information to me. Through our correspondence, I could see that his English was better than my Italian, but it wasn't great. I was often concerned whether we were clear on the arrangements and plans. I'd send five emails to his one, just to be sure.

Now, in the discomfort of my coach seat, I prayed there really was a man named Lorenzo who had taken my PayPal money and did, indeed, have a bed waiting for me along with an apartment.

I'd arranged with Lorenzo to have a driver meet me at the Florence airport. Now my mind bounced with the possibility of no one being there. Was there a plan B? I hadn't given any thought to a backup plan, so I ran the options through my mind.

I had enough money, so if I arrived and there was no Lorenzo and subsequently no apartment, I would check myself into a hotel for two weeks. I would see everything I wanted to see in Florence, dine out and take long walks, and return home. It wasn't the adventure I was hoping for, but it's one I could use as a backup.

And with that decision made, I was suddenly blinded by the harsh cabin lights coming on. Breakfast was served, even though my internal clock knew it was really three a.m. My mind drifted to the last time I was in the Paris airport and my stomach confirmed that I was not confident in my ability to navigate the airport on my own. I'd been in the Charles de Gaulle Airport a few years before, but now it was all a blur. The egg sandwich that arrived on my tray added to my stomach's flip-flops.

The descent into Paris made my plan seem real, and my energy and determination rose. I'd spent the last three months elevating my ability to meditate and visualize outcomes. I inhaled deeply, then slowly exhaled. I closed my eyes and asked my guardian angels to stay close by and walk with me through the labyrinth that is the Charles de Gaulle Airport and through the next steps. I thought I heard them say, "We've got this handled," but I was on caffeine overload, so I may have been imagining it.

I waited in the open lobby, having passed through security, customs, a train ride, and a long flight of steps, finally boarding the flight to my ultimate destination. I was acutely aware of the cacophony of languages around me and intrigued by the predominately European crowd. I wondered where they were all headed to, and not for the first time that day, I wondered what the hell I was doing.

In the extra-small airplane, my head was bobbing drowsily when the announcement of our final approach into Florence came. My twenty-minute nap was not nearly long enough, and I struggled to open my eyes to look out the window at Florence, Italy. The mid-afternoon sun was blazing brightly, and my breath seemed to catch in anticipation.

I walked out of baggage claim with my two heavily loaded suitcases and spotted him immediately, holding a handwritten placard: CONDIE. I fully exhaled. There was a driver here for me, which meant Lorenzo really did exist!

"Signora Condie?" he asked. My response was a dutiful nod, and he introduced himself as Francesco. I tried to think of which day it was, when I last slept, and how many hours until I could sleep again.

Driving into central Florence, as I soon discovered, is never a straight line or a quick procedure in the middle of the day. Francesco drove slowly through seemingly oblivious crowds and cars moving through the streets. Everything outside my window was lively and loud! Horns were blaring, and a vibrant scene played out for me.

I occasionally looked over to see if Francesco was affected at all by any of it. His demeanor conveyed that this was normal life in his city, while I was thinking it was nothing like the neighborhood I left behind. I was equally intrigued and afraid to step out into it.

As we pulled in to park on via dei Calzaiuoli, I looked up to see the Duomo di Firenze. I couldn't take my eyes off of this magnificent structure, looking like a movie set where the scenery is too large and overshadows everything around it. Michelangelo raced around this church as a child, and the brilliant Brunelleschi designed its dome. And here I was to take it in—5,608 miles and twenty hours later!

I asked Francesco as he pulled up to a tall apartment building if we were here.

"*Si, si, si,*" he answered. As he walked with both of my suitcases, he simultaneously placed a call and lit a cigarette. We escaped the frantic energy of the crowded street through the building's side door and were immediately greeted by a wiry, energetic man who appeared on the landing. He was in a crisp, white, long-sleeved shirt and khaki pants, looking fresh despite the heat. He began a rapid-fire exchange with Francesco, greeted me by name, and introduced himself. Lorenzo!

I reached into my wallet to pay Francesco and added a twenty percent tip. He informed me it was too much. "Take it, please," I told him, mostly because I was too tired to argue, and I turned to follow Lorenzo up four more flights of stairs.

Lorenzo was all business as he explained the different keys for the outside door, door to my floor, and my apartment's door. I smiled wearily and nodded, knowing full well I would remember nothing of this conversation.

Inside my apartment was a swirl of blues, dark wood, and the smell of old books. Lorenzo was animated in his tour of the place, but I was still unprepared when he pulled a bed out from the wall! It was a Murphy bed, and my bedroom was also my living room, study, and dining room.

"*Allora,*" Lorenzo was saying as he began each sentence, moving from the Murphy bed to the large window, the kitchen, and the bathroom. In my haze, I wondered if he thought my name was Lora, not Lisa. I wondered if I should I correct him. Maybe another time, I thought. I didn't have the energy right then. Lorenzo seemed to know the English phrases to explain the basics of my apartment, but often the sentence was completed in Italian. I couldn't complain, as he knew more English than I did Italian, so I continued with the ritual of smiling and nodding.

We sat down at the small table in my bedroom/living room/dining room and went over the paper work. I continued to numbly pay attention until he was interrupted mid-sentence by the jolting sound of the bells from the nearby campanile, Campanile di Giotto, pealing through the open window.

I let out a laugh, as the bells were the most delightful thing I had heard for days and were true confirmation that I was sitting in Florence, Italy!

Armed with my set of keys, explicit instructions that I was not to use the hair dryer when the Barbie-sized washing machine was going, and the knowledge that there was coffee and wine in the kitchen, I pulled my Murphy bed out of the wall to take a seat. Seeing Lorenzo close the door behind him left me keenly aware of just how alone I was.

"I am here," I said out loud. "I made it."

The lilt of Italian was coming up from the street and filtered into my window, along with a stream of warm sunlight. I started to tremble just a little, the way you do right before you launch into a full-throttle sob. But I didn't cry. I didn't dare cry. I knew if I started it would open the flood gates and never end. I was all I had at the moment, and I couldn't collapse into an abyss of fear or weeping. And so I breathed, and I closed my eyes and asked for a sign that I'd done the right thing.

Four

Asking for a sign was nothing new for me. I began a couple of years earlier to ask during meditation for a specific, physical sign that I was heading in the right direction on a certain topic. Inevitably, a white feather would appear as confirmation.

I'm sure the argument could be made that because I was looking for a white feather, I would find one. But given the random and inexplicable ways they appeared to me, I choose to believe that they appear as an assurance that all is well.

My children's biggest concern about my living in Florence was my well-known deficient sense of direction. I defended myself to them, and others, by saying I was born and raised in Utah. I never had to develop that skill, as two mountain ranges framed my home to the east and west, making it almost impossible to lose one's bearings.

But here in Florence was an entirely different setup—and my children worried.

My apartment, adjacent to the Cattedrale of Santa Maria del Fiore, better known as the Duomo, was the best luck ever! Imposing and majestic, the cathedral sprawls over the enormous piazza and is the heart of the city of Florence.

The terracotta dome can be seen from almost anywhere in the city, from both sides of the river. Between the sheer size and the accompanying bells from the campanile, I gathered confidence to step out into my new neighborhood.

Lorenzo gave me a map and circled the three closest grocery stores, as well as the Mercato Centrale, the central market.

Of course I knew that I would be alone on this adventure. That part was going to be the terrifying yet wonderful gift. I had never really been all alone, and now I would add to that being in a foreign country and learning a new language and culture. Unlike the "Cheers" bar, no one in Florence knew my name, and certainly no one would miss me at the end of the day if I failed to return to my apartment. Margherita, who worked for Lorenzo, brought in fresh towels and linens once a week, but other than that, my absence would go unnoticed.

I arranged my language lessons to begin the first of November, so October was mine to discover and explore my new city! Armed with maps and a few new phrases (thank you, Google Translator), I stepped out my door each morning with a route in mind.

The luxury of time was exhilarating! I gave myself this gift to uncover a new city that fascinated me in a way I couldn't explain. It called me like a lover, and in complete infatuation, I was head over heels for Florence.

After a lifetime of partnerships, children, jobs, clients, and students, I wondered just how good keeping my own company would be. Would the fact that I knew entire soliloquies from *Camelot* and *Carousel* be enough to keep me entertained, or would they eventually drive me mad?

Striking up conversations with others was pretty much out of the question, as my Italian was limited to saying hello and ordering wine. I observed rather than interacted, took in the sensory heaven that is Florence, and suspiciously eyed the rail-thin Italian girls consuming pastries with their morning's cappuccino.

Throngs of beautiful Italians walked by me every day, in their painted-on jeans and gorgeous leather coats. The women were stunning as they rode bicycles or Vespas in stiletto heels while talking on their cell phones or smoking. Stay-at-home fathers tended to their small children, and kissing couples were everywhere. PDA was obviously not frowned upon here!

Art exhibits and musicians rotated through the main piazzas, providing me with endless entertainment, and I was studying at night to prepare for the next day's adventure. I wanted to dig deeper and know more about the art I was seeing. I realized I knew nothing of the history of Florence, and my lack of education seemed glaring.

Quietly, alone in my small apartment, I studied for the sheer joy of learning. I wrote emails to friends trying to describe all that I was absorbing, but the words weren't conveying it well. There was no way to describe the exhilaration I felt each morning for a new day in Florence!

And I was learning to be alone.

Would I discover after another month or so alone that I had endless capacity to think and create, or would I curl up in utter despair at having to spend another day in my own company?

While my initial plan was to walk in small circles around the block where my apartment was so I could find my way home each time, I found that was unnecessary. My familiarity with the city seemed uncanny. I didn't get lost! I meandered through back streets that wound and curved slowly around, but I always had a sense of where I was. My feet developed calluses from the miles I put on them, and I was grateful for my years of fitness training. Florence is a walking city.

I knew pickpockets were a problem, but the city felt so safe, and I explored both sides of the Arno River, up to San Miniato al Monte, down to Cascine Park, and in every space in between. One night I watched a woman duck behind an ambulance van to change into her "costume" of a poor, pregnant woman. Full on theater, right outside my front door!

I collapsed into my bed at night exhausted but ecstatic. I slept until the bells woke me at seven in the morning; their sound had me smiling before my eyes even opened. I was in Florence!

Five

I was now living very small, and not just in terms of apartment size. While I realized I must travel back to the U.S. in less than three months with only two suitcases, each weighing less than fifty pounds, it was actually my fear of spending too much money that kept me living tightly.

I had the money from the sale of my home and possessions to dip into each month, but I knew that was meant for a down payment on another home eventually. I was receiving a small amount each month from my ex-husband, John, despite my repeated requests to settle for a lump sum, but it was enough to cover rent and utilities for my apartment. All other expenditures would dip into my savings, and I needed to keep that to a minimum.

I had no long-term strategy. I didn't know if Italy would be my forever home, home for a year, or home for just these three months. I did know that, if I wished to live here longer than three months at a time, I needed to obtain a visa from the U.S. and a *Permesso di soggiorno* from Italy. Thinking of either only brought out the Scarlett O'Hara in me—surely I could think about that tomorrow.

Less than two weeks into my stay, however, I replaced the tiny Moka maker with a gigantic one. Espresso is made in a Moka, and given that it's to be consumed in two swallows, it does not require a lot of water!

Given my desire to live frugally, I balked for a few days on buying a coffeemaker and not using the Moka already in my rental kitchen. But as my great-grandmother said after crossing the Atlantic Ocean and then walking with a handcart to Utah, "One can only make so many sacrifices." She, too, had liked her coffee and didn't give a damn that her new religion forbade it! I set out to make my first appliance purchase.

Most store owners in central Florence speak some English, but not a lot and not always happily. No matter; it was not difficult to point to the jumbo-sized Moka maker and say, "Yes!"

Paying cashiers was always a terrifying moment for me. If they said the total in Italian, I didn't understand it, and so I generally pulled out my trusty ATM twenties and tried to estimate how many. The cashier at the store where I was purchasing the Moka maker showed me the receipt, making the transaction easy, and I skipped all the way home thinking of my full pot of coffee in the morning.

It was an exquisite October day—blue sky and very warm. I turned on the air-conditioning, as Lorenzo showed me, and started up a very small load of wash. Feeling pleased with the productive morning, I headed out the door and around the corner to Piazza della Repubblica. I stopped on the way for a well-deserved gelato and headed to my favorite people-watching rest stop.

The piazza was quiet, and the usually crowded bench had several open spots. I sat down to gaze up at the magnificent sky and over to the carousel. It was hard to determine which made me more joyful—the gelato or the views—and I was lost in my own world of happiness when I caught a glimpse of a man from the corner of my eye. He stormed across the piazza yelling, "Signora, signora!" and stopped directly in front of me. My blank face told him everything he needed to know.

"You speak English?" he asked with a heavy accent.

I nodded.

"Madam, you are in the middle of a movie set. May I kindly ask you to move?"

And with that, I noticed for the first time the cameras at the other end of the square and the actors sitting next to me. Apologetically I exited the movie set, finished my gelato, and decided I was probably in need of some socialization. My only saving grace was that no one here knew me, nor would ever see me again, and that provided a small amount of comfort to my embarrassment.

I entered my apartment, flipped on the light switch, and—nothing. I walked into the kitchen to check the Barbie-sized washer; that had come to a stop as well. No power. I sent a text to Lorenzo, who had insisted I have a cell phone, and I was thinking he probably regretted that.

Five minutes later there was a knock at the door. I opened it, expecting to see one of the few familiar faces I knew, and instead there stood a small Italian woman with a very serious demeanor.

In broken English she managed to let me know that I'd blown the power by using the air-conditioning at the same time as the washer. She ended by saying, "Don't do that again," and I nodded as I accepted my scolding.

Given the events of the morning, I decided to spend the afternoon safely in my apartment, reading.

That night after the campanile bells had struck for the last time that day, I reached over to turn off the light. Something caught my eye. It was a small, perfectly white feather sitting alone on the nightstand, just beyond the base of the lamp. I smiled, thanked my angels, and said good night. Apparently they have a sense of humor.

I decided to join a tour with a local company—Walkabout Florence. They took English-speaking groups to Siena, San Gimignano, and Pisa all in one day, and it sounded perfect to me. I realized once my language classes began, I wouldn't have as much freedom to travel during the week.

It was a fantastic day, and conversations in English were a welcome respite. Having been to Pisa before and climbed the leaning tower on my initial trip to Italy at age seventeen, I opted to sit down and watch the sun set.

An American woman from the tour plopped down beside me. "Are you traveling alone?" she asked. "My friend and I noticed you earlier today."

"Actually, I'm living in Florence," I answered, and we introduced ourselves.

"Well, then," Jan said, "you must meet my friend, Nancy. She's an amazing woman, and she just moved here too. You'll love her!"

"Okay," I said, not too convinced.

Five minutes later, Nancy joined us, and we arranged for the three of us to meet for lunch next week. Jan was visiting for just a couple of weeks and wanted to know if I had any interest in joining her for another tour with Walkabout Florence. They offered a full day of hiking in the Cinque Terre, and while I had heard about this area, I was not exactly sure what I was signing up for. Nevertheless, I said yes to joining her on Saturday for the tour.

As I walked back from the bus station to my tiny home in my new city, I gazed up at the Duomo, with its white-and-green marble. The moon hanging just between the campanile and the massive church made it look like a photograph. I was overcome with gratitude again at the forces that propelled me to this new country and new life.

I said yes to things outside my comfort zone, and the rewards arrived. I had a friend in Florence and a plan for another adventure.

Six

My days were filled with going to the markets, exploring, writing correspondence, and now, spending time with a few friends. After meeting Nancy, a circle of expats seemed to open up. I signed up for weekly walking tours from Alexandra Lawrence, American-born but living now in Florence. She was charming and knowledgeable, and the Florence expats knew her tours were a must and signed up early. Rarely did I join one and not end up going to coffee or lunch with a few people, so my need for socialization was quickly met. Expats were a friendly, inclusive group, as most had come to Italy not knowing many people. We needed each other!

I still had hours on end of time alone, and I researched and studied all the main attractions of my new city. After checking off a good many, I decided to explore the church up high on a hill overlooking all of Florence. I'd read about San Miniato, and that it provided one of the most spectacular views in the city. The story is that San Miniato, or Saint Minias, was an Armenian prince serving in the Roman Army. After becoming a hermit, he was denounced as a Christian and brought before the Emperor Decius, who was outside the gates of Florence. Beheaded in front of the Emperor, Saint Minias picked up his own head, crossed the Arno River and walked up the steep hill to his hermitage. Sounds believable to me! After a shrine was erected on the spot, a chapel was built in the eighth century.

Crossing over the Arno River on Ponte alle Grazie, I paused to look at the water's reflection. Shimmering images in varying golds and grays, I realized that there was absolutely nothing familiar about this landscape to me, and yet I felt so at home. The colors of the buildings matched the leaves on the trees and ground, and I marveled that perhaps October is beautiful everywhere. I pulled my scarf in a little tighter around my neck, agreeing with the Italians that a cold neck is the root of all illness, and turned left at San Niccolò.

Walking through the archway of the ancient wall that remained, I began the climb up the narrow street and followed the signs for the church. Seeing the flights of stairs ahead, I was reminded of my twenty years of teaching step aerobics. I felt I was well equipped for the challenge and began my way up the wide, tree-lined course. Three-quarters of the way up, my calves were screaming with pain! I stopped and pretended to take in the beauty of the view as I dropped each heel, one at a time, off the step to stretch. Was it the altitude, or was I *that* out of shape?

Following the several flights of stairs up to the doorway, I entered the church of San Miniato. The frescoed walls, with their deep reds and oranges, surrounded the benches, and I quickly took a seat, needing to catch my breath. My lungs were screaming, and I decided a somber, prayerful countenance might buy me some sitting time to recoup. Looking up, I saw the gold glitter of the mosaic of Christ between the Virgin and Saint Minias, made in 1260. I gazed up at the wooden beams overhead and thought of my country. *Fourteen-hundred and ninety-two, Columbus sailed the ocean blue.* I couldn't fathom that all this architecture was in place decades before my country had even been discovered. And, as I did once a day, I took it all in and said quietly under my breath, "Clearly I'm not in Kansas anymore."

Make peace with silence, and remind yourself that it is in this space that you'll come to remember your spirit. When you're able to transcend an aversion to silence, you'll also transcend many other miseries.

—Dr. Wayne Dyer

Quietly I sat in the cavernous space of San Miniato, hearing only the occasional footsteps of another person. Inside the church was cold, but I was warm from walking, and I deeply inhaled the incense-infused air. My soul was filled with gratitude for the gift, again, of having the time to "transcend an aversion to silence," and as I sat, I said a prayer of gratitude.

I found a new place to people-watch while I ate lunch. While All'Antico Vinaio was the most famous lunch spot, I found several spots that I thought were equally as good. I favored the ones where the sandwiches are listed by number, and I could ask for that, rather than pointing to each item and asking for this or that. *Panino* in hand, I headed down to via Tornabuoni and sat out on built-in benches of the palazzo.

This was California's Rodeo Drive of Florence; beautiful people and expensive shopping, and the people-gazing was extraordinary! Businessmen of every age, in gorgeous suits, walked by with equally striking women who apparently didn't get the memo that fur was no longer stylish. Everything they wore was exquisite, and the elegance that the Italian people seem to be given at birth was artwork in itself.

I finished my *panino* but sat a bit longer to ponder the important questions:

How is it that a woman's leg can be the same circumference from the knee to the thigh? And, how the hell did she get into those jeans?

Is there a beauty component required of policemen before they qualify to wear those fabulous blue uniforms (designed by Farragamo)?

Why are these people in down jackets and furs when it's 68 degrees Fahrenheit?

How much further do I need to walk to earn another gelato?

Seven

November arrived in Florence with slightly cooler temperatures and a little rain. I was grateful for both, as well as the crowds that seemed to have disappeared in one day. Streets were wider, piazzas almost empty, and there never was a line at a museum or exhibit.

I spent a day with *David*, as in Michelangelo's masterpiece at the Galleria dell'Accademia. The throngs of admirers were gone, and I leisurely gazed up at the statue from every angle. I was aware of the gaping hole in my education where art history should have been. I was envious of the schoolchildren I saw out on field trips in Florence, strolling nonchalantly through world-renowned museums and galleries.

It was a magnificent afternoon with *David* and once again a surreal experience to think that, at least for another two months, this was my life. I lived here, and this was how I filled my days!

The next day I began language class at Istituto Italiano. I had heard about this school on my last full day in Rome in June of 2012. When I entered the dining room of the bed and breakfast where my daughter and I had been staying at, I heard two men speaking what I presumed to be Italian. I hunted for something besides cake or yogurt, took a roll and a cup of coffee, and sat down across from them at the long table.

"Where are you from?" one of the men asked, looking up from their conversation. I noticed how handsome they both were.

"Utah," I answered, wishing I'd taken the time to put on make-up. "I thought you were Italian," I added.

They were American, I found out, both working for a tour company and studying Italian in Florence. I told them that I was envious, as I had fallen in love with Italy, and their Italian had fooled me! They were leaving that day for the U.S. but told me that if I ever wanted to take Italian in Italy, I should go to Florence. Their school was Istituto Italiano, and they highly recommended it.

I laughed a little as I thanked them. Italian lessons in Italy—as if I'd ever need that advice!

That morning, as I walked down via Martelli, I was reminded of the serendipity that led me to this school: a chance conversation one morning over coffee that preceded my decision to move to Italy by only twenty-four hours. I hadn't thought to ask them for a card or their names, but I mentally thanked them as I located the school's address on the side of an impressive building near the Duomo.

I had been in contact with several of the personnel who worked there, as they had given me Lorenzo's information, and we communicated on starting dates and payments. Payment in full was to be made on the first morning—in cash. No exceptions.

I was excited to begin learning Italian, as I knew it would be necessary. I'd observed Americans speaking Italian *to* Italians, and I could see that it was appreciated. Playing charades at the market was not what I wanted to do, and if this was to be more than an extended visit, I needed to be able to speak some Italian.

I was terrified.

I didn't know a language other than English. I took French in junior high, and it was a total bust.

Istituto Italiano sounded impressive—even daunting. Had they ever had a student as old as me? Had their highly touted immersion process ever not succeeded? Would the cool kids let me sit at their table?

Eight

To reach the school, I walked for about two minutes across the piazza and in between the Florence Baptistery and the Duomo. I couldn't resist looking up! Remembering my trip to San Miniato, I opted for the four flights of stairs instead of the tiny elevator once I entered the building.

I hiked up the final flight, gasping only a little. I gathered my courage and resolved to face this challenge with enthusiasm rather than fear. When I looked down on the last of the steps, I saw it. Laying pristine on the red carpet was a feather—a single white feather—that told me I was not walking these steps alone, and I was on the right path.

The first five minutes of class answered several questions. I was the oldest student, by far. I'm guessing I had a decade on the teacher. There was only one long table in the center of the room, so all the "kids" sat at the same one—cool or not.

None of my earlier concerns were what I was thinking about, however. The teacher asked students to stand, introduce themselves, and say where they are from…in Italian.

Wait. Wasn't this the Beginning 1 class? How was it that each person was standing up, saying *Sono* and their name, and rattling off other information in Italian? The teacher was speaking only in Italian, and everyone else seemed to be following along.

Coffee break, or *pausa*, came after two hours of class and not a moment too soon for me. I bee-lined it to the office and told the secretary, Francesca, that I was going to need a tutor.

With a patronizing smile, she let me know that all new students feel a bit overwhelmed the first day, and if I kept at it, I'd be fine.

I offered a patronizing smile right back, knowing now why they required payment in full before classes began, and told her, "No. I need a tutor, and I am happy to pay for one."

Francesca sighed heavily and picked up the phone that resulted in several minutes of rapid Italian and more deep sighs. All I understood from her side of the conversation was my name. Placing the phone down, she walked away, and I wondered if our conversation was over.

A few minutes later, Francesca returned to tell me that the director will be making the decision as to whether or not I could have a tutor, and they would let me know before tomorrow's class. *Really?*

Later that evening, while eating dinner in my apartment, I heard the email notification on my iPad. The school confirmed that the director found someone willing to take on the task of being my tutor. I would begin the next afternoon with Signora Barbara, who I could only pray had the patience of Job.

Signora Barbara Cipriani was a classic Florentine woman. Warm, chocolate-colored eyes and long, curly black hair; her face was welcoming, but all business. I introduced myself in English, and she did the same, and then she announced that we were to speak only Italian. I was guessing I wouldn't be very chatty in this class!

I was meeting with Barbara every day for two hours and found that she was, indeed, the Miracle Worker. Kind, but very firm and direct, I think she was a bit surprised to find that I had absolutely no foundation in a foreign language from which we would build upon.

We began with flashcards, just as I had taught my children. I'd picked up some basics in the month I'd been in Florence, such as colors, foods, and numbers. But she moved on to verbs, and I was studying fervently each night.

It wasn't enough for Signora Barbara that I knew the words. She wanted me to understand that Italian was sung as much as it was spoken. The cadence and rhythm were what made it flow, with vowels drawn out and consonants ignored. Praise was hard won from my teacher, but when it came, my name had three syllables.

"*Brava, Leeeeeza,*" she said as I mimicked her pronunciation of a sentence. I beamed like a five-year-old.

This was a whole new world for me. I could walk into a ballet or fitness class and be at home anywhere in the world. But in an Italian 1 language class, I was stymied. It was humbling, frustrating, and only occasionally rewarding, but I was determined to get whatever I could out of the next six weeks of class. I realized that at no time in my life did I ever think I'd need to know Italian, and the one advantage in knowing nothing is that anything is an improvement!

Signora Barbara recommended that I turn on the television at night, just to tune my ear to the sound of the language. I tried to do it, but it made my head hurt, and I was exhausted with Italian and anyone who spoke it.

My head hit the pillow, and I immediately started to sink into sleep. I heard Barbara's voice singing in my head. I heard her coaching me as I completed my homework each night, and I heard her now, whispering as I drifted off, exhausted.

Nine

Structure was not a bad feature to add to my days, which became a bit more predictable. Mornings found me in class, then *caffè macchiato* at eleven o'clock, lunch generally with friends, and a few hours of studying at night.

My studying often wandered from language to art to history, but all of it revolved around Italy—primarily Florence. I was captivated by my new home!

Weekends were for traveling, and I could usually find someone willing to take a day's adventure with me. Often, we wouldn't know exactly which destination we were headed for until we got to the kiosk at the train station and checked out the times and prices.

One Sunday I met Nancy for a return trip to Pietrasanta. We both wanted more time in this community, which was filled with artisans, studios, and sculptures. Last time we visited, a gentleman had invited us into his studio, where we watched him work on a masterpiece of mosaic. These were my favorite days, where we had a general plan but no timetable.

The conductor announced our arrival in Pietrasanta, and Nancy and I jumped up and headed for the door. The train squealed to a stop, but the door refused to open. I tried again to no avail and moved aside to let Nancy give it a go. We quickly decided to make a run to the next car to try that door, knowing the stops didn't last long on the regional trains.

Just as I grabbed the door's handle, the train pulled away. After a minute of assessing our choices, Nancy and I decided we would get off at the next stop, wherever that may be, and take the train back to Pietrasanta. The next stop came quickly, the door opened, and out we went. Forte dei Marmi-Seravezza-Querceta. Never heard of it!

Looking around, we realized we leaped long before we looked! There was no real station here—more of a drop-off point, and nobody else around. It was a Sunday afternoon, and this place, wherever we were, was quiet. Looking at the train schedule, we saw we had a bit of a wait to catch the next train heading to Pietrasanta, so we made a quick decision to explore this town and, since it was close to noon, to find a place for lunch.

All of the stores were closed, and we were mostly wandering through residential streets with an occasional car wash or bar open. I realized it was going to be up to me to ask for directions. I was hardly better than no help at all, but I could put a few Italian words together to at least find out where we were and where we might go to eat.

As we wandered into the bar, there was no question that Nancy and I were outsiders. Four young men and a woman were hanging out over coffee, and it was hard to determine who worked there and who was a customer.

We stood at the counter and waited until a handsome young man with black curly hair and baggy jeans asked us, in Italian, what we would like.

"Um, *dove siamo?*" I asked. His face registered surprise and confusion. I'd just asked him where we were.

"*Scusate, signore, non ho capito,*" he replied. He didn't understand, and his eyes seem to be asking if I was teasing or not.

"*Dove siamo?*" I asked again, because I hadn't the words to explain that we were sincere in not knowing where we were. We did a few more rounds of basically the same dialogue, when finally he seemed to understand. I wasn't crazy—just lost.

The young barista wrote *QUERCETA* on a napkin and handed it to me. He looked up at his friends to see if they were watching the spectacle as I ordered a *caffè macchiato* and Nancy ordered *l'aqua frizzante*. We took our drinks out the front of the bar where two small tables were set up. There were no cars on the road, and no one walked by. I started to wonder if we'd drifted into the Twilight Zone.

I was going to ask the barista where we would find a good place to eat, now that we knew where we were, but I felt I'd pushed my luck with him about as far as it would go, so Nancy and I headed out across the street.

Walking toward what appeared to be the center of town, if there was one, Nancy spotted a woman about our age getting in a car.

"Her! Go ask her where we can find a restaurant," Nancy said. Humans were hard to spot here, so I agreed.

By the time I reached the car, the woman was inside and had started the engine. She lowered the window about halfway to hear what I was after.

I asked in my best (but probably awful) Italian where we could find a good restaurant for lunch, and she began peppering me with rapid Italian as I struggled to pull out a word or two that I knew.

This lovely woman was dressed for church, Sunday dinner, or both, but she let me know that nothing would be open until at least one o'clock for lunch. She recommended a place just around the corner, up the street, first left, down the street, second right—or something. I nodded as I said, "*Si, si, si, e grazie mille*," as I backed away and allowed her to pull into the street.

"So, where are we going?" Nancy asked as we started to walk.

"I have no idea," I answered, "but apparently there is a very good restaurant in this town, so let's start walking."

One fantastic meal later, surrounded by large parties of Italian families, we were stuffed and happy. It may not have been the place we'd been directed to, but it was a find! Small pitchers of red wine, stained from years of use, red and white cloth napkins and complimentary *limoncello* added to our lively mood, and off we headed to the train station.

Serendipity had planned a perfect Sunday afternoon of dining and exploring in the late autumn sunshine. I leaned my head back on the blue vinyl seat of the train and closed my eyes as we careened back to Florence. My memories were full of Sunday dinners with family around a table of pot roast, homemade rolls, and love. As much as I missed all of that, time moved on and, happily, so had I.

Ten

For such a small apartment, I had a rather large window that took up most of one wall. The view down was nothing to look at, but the view upward always took my breath away! Beautiful blue skies, drifting clouds, and cool air welcomed me as I hung my head out to check the weather and on my clothes drying on the outside line.

One advantage of such tight quarters was that I heard others' voices and music through my window, and it made me feel less alone. The familiar clatter of dishes and the lilting Italian reassured me that I had neighbors, even if I didn't know them. Often, when hanging my head out the window, I'd looked up or down on neighboring faces, but waving did not garner me any new friends, and so I quit.

Tonight a glorious aria drifted through my main room and into the kitchen where I was chopping and dicing broccoli, peppers, and onions. I found that dinner could be made at home for next to nothing, and the ingredients were fresh from the outdoor market or my local *fruttivendolo*.

As I inhaled the fragrance of the new olive oil drizzled over the vegetables, I sat down to read my evening's emails. Given the time change, most of my messages from the U.S. arrived about dinnertime and made for perfect companionship while I ate.

I saw an email from Thomas, my on-again-off-again partner in Utah, and I girded myself up to read his email. Since I had made the decision to move to Italy the previous June and left him behind on the trip prior to the decision, our relationship had been tenuous. Rather than finalizing the break-up once and for all, we apparently thought the same argument needed another hundred go-rounds.

My feelings were mixed on reading his words. While comforting in familiarity, they seemed to be from another world away—another lifetime. They made me uncomfortable in the way my soul spoke when I knew the ending had already happened, but I hadn't had the strength to face it yet. I knew my heart had closed that chapter of my life.

Mixed with the daily events of his week came the requests to please stay in touch more, please don't leave him out of the loop, and please don't forget him. I moved to the next email.

Lorenzo wrote, even though he lived just across the hall, and his message was all in Italian. Running it through Google Translate left me laughing, but understanding that a woman had arrived in our apartment building from Mexico City. She spoke English, but her luggage did not arrive with her. Lorenzo asked me to stop by and introduce myself to her tomorrow. Her apartment was just down the hall from mine.

Most of Lorenzo's apartments were rented by the week, so I had become a bit of a fixture while staying for two months. I had to call Lorenzo at least once a week for assistance with something, and despite that (or perhaps because of it) we became good friends. He enjoyed my attempts to speak Italian and asked me to join him on occasion when a new English-speaking guest arrived. He was animated, laughed easily, and was a perfectionist when it came to cleanliness of his apartments. He wanted his English-speaking guests to feel comfortable, concerned on occasion if he couldn't understand all their needs. I, yet again, felt the good fortune of serendipity, which had led me to my first Italian friend.

After my class ended the next day, I headed straight back to my building and knocked on the apartment two doors down from mine. I was about to decide that the new tenant was not there when a woman opened the door. It was one o'clock in the afternoon, yet I had obviously awakened her. I apologized and told her I would return later. Anyone who flies internationally knows that there is no shame in sleeping into late afternoon when you've just arrived! She insisted I come in, saying that she needed to get up.

I sat down in her apartment, which was even smaller than mine, and marveled that that was even possible. She was wrapped up in a white robe, hair disheveled, no makeup, and still one of the most beautiful women I had ever seen. I watched as she tried to focus her eyes and wake up. We laughed, as we got through our introductions, at our palatial living accommodations and our friendly landlord. I introduced myself as Victoria told me that her luggage still hadn't arrived, so I offered to bring her some shampoo, conditioner, soap, and toothpaste, along with a change of clothing, so she could get a shower and feel like a lady. She agreed on one condition: that she take me to dinner the following night to thank me. It was a date!

Victoria's luggage arrived the next day, and we met at the restaurant just around the corner from our apartment building. I was, again, stunned by how beautiful she was. While Italian women typically dress in classic black, Victoria from Mexico City was a sight to behold in her gold, green, and aqua blue ensemble! She welcomed me like I was a long-lost friend and, over a bottle of Chianti and some melt-in-my-mouth *tagliatelle bolognese*, we bonded. We told each other our brief stories about how it is we had come to live in tiny apartments on via Calzaiuoli, in Florence, Italy. We toasted to a lasting friendship and walked arm-in-arm back to our apartments.

Eleven

Thanksgiving

While my friends and family in the U.S. had the day off for Thanksgiving, I was seated at a local *trattoria* with five other women for our celebration. It was complete with steaming bowls of pasta, pitchers of Chianti, and new friendship. Our group came from Canada, Mexico, and the United States for a nontraditional Thanksgiving dinner, and I found myself feeling richly surrounded by fascinating company and plentiful plates of food.

I was grateful.

I thought that day would bring some melancholy moments of feeling far away from those I loved and the time-honored traditions of my life, but it did not. I mourned the losses of family life, as I had once known it years ago. I mourned the inevitable end with Thomas, but none of it made me sad that day.

Sometimes I longed for the safety of that life, the knowledge of how I would spend Sundays and where Christmas Eve would be, but I was trying to loosen my grip on those reins and allow a new life to unfold.

I was content to know that those I loved had plans today, and it all went on without me, half a world away. I'd had a chance to Skype with my two children, Justin and Lauren, and they were together and encouraging. They reminded me that I would be back in Utah in one month, and my stomach dropped a little.

I left the group after dinner and walked alone along the Arno River. I crossed Ponte alle Grazie and looked across the river to the Uffizi Gallery. Shrouded in clouds, the moon offered little light, but the lights that lined the river cast a yellow glow on the water.

I allowed my mind to briefly drift back to a long dining room table, set with Lenox china and crystal, complete with a traditional menu and a traditional family—a scene that although didn't still exist didn't make me any less proud that it did at one time. I was the hub of my family, the nurturer and holiday planner, in a role that I didn't ever see ending. But it did end, and now I was a woman wrapped in a scarf and heavy coat who walked alone by the Arno River.

I crossed one of the most famous bridges in the world, Ponte Vecchio, and stopped in the middle to gaze west. That time of year, the crowds were gone, the ancient shops lining the bridge were boarded up early, and I was almost alone on this famous, remarkable landmark. I wondered about the Florentines in centuries past who walked across this bridge and watched the sun set. Every night was a picture perfect moment from this spot.

I looked above to the Vasari Corridor and imagined ghosts peering through the small, round windows to see the populace going by. I wondered if Adolf Hitler's direct order, which preserved only this bridge in Florence, was because he loved art, or because they needed the passageway from Rome into the city.

There was a bit of an eerie feel to this part of Florence when the shops were closed and the bridge damp with rain. But I was never afraid to walk in my city at any time of the day or night.

"Happy Thanksgiving," I said softly to myself. It's one I never saw coming, but one I'll never forget; my first Thanksgiving outside the United States was on my own.

I felt the love of my children and friends reach across the ocean, and as I continued on this journey, I felt their support and caring. I might have been on my own, but I was not alone.

Twelve

A small flip calendar left by a former occupant of my apartment now served as a daily reminder that it was December, and I would be going back to Utah on Christmas Day.

I pulled on my boots to head out to school. Just looking at the date that morning made tears well up in my eyes. I was not ready to be back in Utah. The thought of it made my body feel heavy and my chest feel tight. The only word I could think of was dread. I was filled with dread to have to return.

I became an expert observer during my two months there. I eavesdropped at any occasion to pick up the gist of an Italian conversation and told myself it was all in the name of studying. I was getting past the "deer in the headlights" moments and could comfortably speak a few words in Italian when it was my turn in the market, and I was beginning to recognize, if not understand, some of the Italian culture.

Italian culture seemed to me to be a paradox. The entire country *appeared* to have no rules, and yet, it did indeed have very stringent rules—just not the rules I was raised with.

Driving rules appeared to not exist, standing in a queue was impossible, and no one waited their turn. But order a cappuccino after noon, and observe the barista's face. Go outside with wet hair or without a scarf, and several people will inform you of the danger. And, in a country where the population is overwhelmingly Catholic, condoms are sold by vending machine and available 24-7.

Fashion, food, and digestion all had strict rules, and for the most part, I happily embraced them.

I was just starting to hit my stride in my city, with this culture, but now my days in Florence were winding down. I reminded myself that the time in Utah would only be the required three months, as I was determined to return to Florence. I was studying online forums and reading how to apply for a visa and *Permesso di soggiorno*, and the conversation among my expat friends often revolved around this subject. Some had been successful; others not. I likened my chances to that of Charlie winning a golden ticket to Willy Wonka's chocolate factory, but I was going to try. While there were some in the group who overstayed the ninety days allowed without a visa, I knew I wouldn't do well if I were here illegally. The punishment could be a one-to-three-year ban from the Schengen Union, of which Italy is a part, and that would break my heart.

I felt my stomach lurch whenever I thought about applying for a visa. I wasn't coming to Italy for a job or with a husband; I would be asking to live in this country because I loved it here, and there's not a box on the application for that.

As I walked to school, I passed in front of the Duomo, looked up at the glistening marble, and smiled. Surely the angels that had helped me this far wouldn't let me down now! I counted off to myself all the ways I was ingrained in my new city as I climbed the flights of stairs to my school. I had a hair stylist who ignored any instruction I gave him but who created a wonderful new look for me. I had the trusty expat doctor, Dr. Kerr, to go to if I was sick. I was a recognized face at the bar on the corner between my school and apartment, and the barista knew I'd order a *caffè macchiato*, just as I knew his wife would start yelling at him from the back if our conversation lasted more than a few minutes.

I had Lorenzo and his lovely wife, Letizia, who invited me into their home and took me with them to the country. By a great stroke of luck, Signora Barbara was teaching the beginner Italian class when I signed up for the new month, so my Italian was coming along. My life felt like it was flowing in a daily rhythm, and I was becoming a part of the city.

On December 8, after a gathering of my expat girlfriends for *aperitivo*, we joined the rest of the citizens of Florence in front of the Duomo where the lights of the Christmas tree would be lit. This event signaled the beginning of the holiday season, and it was a refreshing change to not have Christmas begin any earlier like it does in the States.

As the greetings were made over the loudspeaker, I looked around at the crowd. Small children on their parents' shoulders, everyone wrapped in heavy scarves, hats, gloves, and jackets, there was a feeling of festivity in the air that night as neighbors and families gathered. That day at school, a few snowflakes were seen through the window, causing the class to stop and rush out to look. It was December—lovely with its understated elegance and simplicity.

As the community counted down to the lighting, we joined in: "*Cinque, Quattro, Tres, Due, Uno!*" and the enormous tree, dwarfed only in comparison to the Duomo, was washed with light. With cheers from the crowds and music playing, our group moved toward the tree where we each took a photo among the red gillie ornaments, the fleur-de-lis–shaped symbols of Florence.

I realized I was looking at Florence through the innocence of an outsider. I had fallen in love a few times in my life, and I recognized the symptoms. I accepted that I was guilty as charged, happily walking on air as I learned more about this ancient city that held me for the past three months and allowed me to grow more solid, more sure of myself.

I was to leave on Christmas morning for Utah and, through the magic of time zones, arrive in Salt Lake City on Christmas afternoon! All my shopping was done in Florence at the markets and artisans' shops where I hoped to find a bit of classic Italian gifting to my friends and family.

I said goodbye to my classmates and my teacher, Barbara, and made the rounds to say goodbye to those I knew in Florence. Some of the expats would be here when I returned in March, but many would not be. It was strange to have forged such strong bonds of friendship in so little time, as we came together in a country where we were outsiders. It was a great comfort to have this network of people who came into my life in a thousand random ways.

———— ————

It was four-thirty a.m. on Christmas morning, and I stood outside with my luggage on via dei Calzaiuoli. Lorenzo called the previous night to arrange for a taxi, and now I gazed down the empty street and prayed one was coming. I looked to my left at the Duomo, magnificent in the early-morning moonlight, and I promised her I'd return.

The night before, several of us attended a midnight mass where a cardinal joined the congregation. Amid the pageantry and ritual, the incense and Italian, I felt I had come home. Never in my wildest dreams did I think life would have reserved a seat for me, on Christmas Eve, in the Duomo, the Cattedrale di Santa Maria del Fiore of Florence, Italy. It was just another of the magical memories I would carry with me as I flew across the ocean.

Silence was broken when the taxi turned the corner and headed toward me. The headlights glared through the darkened street, and my heart leapt at knowing I was on my way! When I climbed in the backseat, I was excited for the first time about making this trip. Justin and Lauren were at the other end of this journey! I couldn't wait to see my kids!

———— ————

There really are no words for the sensation of hugging my children after not seeing them for months. Soul of my soul they are, and we laughed, talked, ate, and opened gifts on Christmas Day. Thankfully, they understood when seven o'clock arrived and I exited to bed.

Thirteen

January 2013

With my least favorite month of the year half over, I was busy in Utah, lunching with friends and teaching some classes again at my old gym. It was nice to reconnect, good to catch up, but my head and heart were elsewhere.

There was no way for me to describe my daily life in Florence to my friends and family, and I could tell by their questions that most didn't understand. "Aren't you lonely?" was the most common, with "When are you moving back?" at a close second. I could tell some were concerned, perplexed, and wondering if I'd gone off the deep end. Those who knew me well could tell that I was enthusiastic and content with my decision. *And no, I'm not moving back*, I would think to myself.

I had seen Thomas, even stayed with Thomas because, apparently, I have no spine when it comes to saying goodbye to a man. But after I spent the night lying awake, terrified he was going to hurt me again, I knew I had no other choice but to go. The difference this time—it was for good. No cat-and-mouse email, call on occasion, or let's stay friends, providing a big safety net. I had tried a thousand ways to bend this relationship into something it would never be, and it was time—past time—to walk away.

In just three months in Florence, I had come to know some truths about my deepest desires, and I began to understand the unyielding force that pulled me to Italy. I chose experiences over possessions. I was still choosing the thrill of not knowing what's around the corner over the stagnant life I had been living. I redefined every day what mattered most to me, and I stood on my own two feet while doing it. And I was doing it all without a man accompanying me. I stepped so far out of my comfort zone that appearing foolish didn't even faze me. I was at the mercy of strangers every day with a myriad of questions and a curiosity that continued to expand.

Sleeping on a futon in my daughter's condo felt fine to me if it meant I could return to Florence. I did not miss my "stuff" or any of its weight at all. Because I knew the dance steps so well, I could easily go through the motions of daily life in the U.S., but I missed the sensory overload of Italy.

Early in January, I received the distressing news that I needed surgery to repair and replace the tear duct on my left eye. I'd been bothered with overflowing tears for months and was hopeful there would be a quick fix to the problem once I saw a doctor in the U.S.

As the doctor explained the details of the surgery and recovery, I couldn't imagine such a small body part could cause so much grief. The good news, however, was that I was scheduled for surgery the first week of February, so I would be able to fly by March 25.

I lay on my back staring straight up at the ceiling. I had been, historically, a terrible patient, and this time was no different. I had imagined healing time would find me curled up with a blanket and a good book, but my one good eye didn't seem to be focusing. TV was annoying to me, so I downloaded all of the Pimsleur Italian courses and listened and repeated as cued. If nothing else, I would not lose the hard-fought progress of my new language!

Sometimes I closed my eyes and quit playing along—to just listen. In my mind, I navigated the narrow streets of my beloved

Florence. I heard the clatter of dishes through the back door of a *trattoria*, or the blaring of opera through my neighbor's window. I imagined walking the steps to San Miniato and, stopping to catch my breath, taking in the view of all five bridges over the Arno. I could see my barista with his hands flying as he tells me a story, and I could almost taste my favorite gelato from Gelato di Filo in San Niccolò.

"Wait for me," I whispered, before the pain pills kicked in and put me to sleep. "I'm coming back."

Fourteen

And if travel is like love, it is, in the end, mostly because it's a heightened state of awareness, in which we are mindful, receptive, undimmed by familiarity and ready to be transformed. That is why the best trips, like the best love affairs, never really end.

—Pico Iyer

Perhaps truly great love affairs never end, but all the ones I'd had in my life had. Taking the last of my possessions from Thomas's condo made that clear. I wouldn't be back, even for a weekend visit. The woman who had left last October wasn't the same woman who returned, and there was no way to pretend she was.

Packing and preparing to return to my little apartment in Florence was easier this time. I knew what was superfluous and what I really needed. Jars of Trader Joe's almond butter were tucked inside pairs of boots. Big bottles of aspirin, Aleve, and multiple vitamins made the trip, as they are dreadfully expensive in Italy. Clinique and Lancome makeup was available in Italy, but also very expensive, so I packed a three-month supply.

Really good walking shoes were a necessity. I bought two additional pairs of my favorite Steve Madden Trooper boots; I wore holes in the ones I took over last fall. Those Italian women navigated the cobblestone streets in high-heeled shoes, but the rest of us were doomed if we tried to copy, so the flat Troopers got to take up highly valuable space.

I didn't realize that some of my friends had been a little worried about me, and it was comforting for them to see that I was thriving and happy. I had no way to describe to them what it was like to wake up to the bells from the nearby campanile, or stand on the bank of the Arno to watch the ethereal clouds swirl in pinks and oranges at sunset. There was no way to let them know the inward pride I felt at such a small feat like ordering my lunch in Italian, or being able to flirt with the *fruttivendolo*! These moments were mine, or ones to share with my Florentine friends, and I realized again what made the expat community so tight. It's the same reason that Chinatown and Little Italy exist in the United States. There are some things that must be shared to fully be understood, and so my expat friends and I carry these sweet memories in my heart.

It was bittersweet to see that life went on in Salt Lake City without me. Of course, time didn't stand still for it or me, but it was odd to have missed holidays and the monthly dinners with my girlfriends, especially the Dodo Girls—Jane Rogers, Jean Mack, Sherrilee Seibert, and Lelan Dianes. We'd shared every major life event together for forty-plus years, and all the not-so-major ones as well! Our friendships had survived distances before, but no one had ever pushed it to my new limit. They reassured me that they would watch over my children, keep me up to date on any news, and start a "Florence Fund" to come see me in the fall.

While many weeks of my time home were spent recovering from the eye surgery, I had time to reconnect with friends, students, and family. I was ready to see the red terracotta roofs of Florence, but saying goodbye to my two children never got easier.

This time arriving at Peretola, the airport in Florence, I didn't have a driver waiting for me. It was a tiny airport, and my biggest struggle was to carve a space through the crowd of Italians who were hovering over the baggage carousel.

"*Scusi, scusi, per favore!*" I worked my way forward after spotting the first of my two suitcases.

Italians don't have the same idea of personal space as Americans do; and being from the western United States, I'm used to even a little extra space! Feeling breath on the back of my neck, I turned around and gave an exasperated look, complete with the hand gesture meaning *What are you doing?* I was tired, I'd been up for twenty-four hours, and I hadn't forgotten how to hold my own in an Italian crowd.

Navigating my suitcases to the taxi stand, I got the next available car and sank into the backseat. It was a warm late afternoon in March, and the noise of the traffic and the blare of the radio welcomed me back. Lorenzo knew my approximate time of arrival, and this time I was not worried that I may not have an apartment. My only worry was I knew that Lorenzo ran on Italian time.

I was greeted by one of Lorenzo's workers who informed me that Lorenzo had gone to his beach house and handed me the keys.

Opening the familiar wooden door to my little apartment felt like I never left. The blue walls and colorful rug greeted me, and I opened the window to let in the warm afternoon air. "*Ciao,*" I said to no one as I lifted the blinds all the way up, catching the rays of sunlight. "*Sono a casa.*"

My two suitcases took up a large part of the floor space, but I realized I didn't need to unpack everything right now. I eyed the inviting Murphy bed in the wall, knowing that if I gave in to sleep now, I'd be awake all night. My back ached and my body begged to stretch out, but I took a shower, put on fresh clothes, and headed out to see my city and find some dinner.

Fifteen

I was back in school, although Signora Barbara was not my teacher this time. The class was international and young, once again, with the exception of my new friend, Peter.

Peter was the only person in the class who was older than I was, which was why I liked him immediately! He was from Great Britain and each day arrived to class dressed in a long-sleeve, button-down shirt and a jacket. He had a full head of white hair and the lightest blue eyes I'd ever seen. His hand trembled just a little, and that day when I sat down next to him, he introduced himself to me in Italian. I was charmed!

Peter told me that he had taken Italian classes at a university for seniors in England. Knowing the only way to improve rapidly was to come to Italy to practice, he asked his wife for a hall pass! I learned that he was eighty-three years old, and he was here on his own for two weeks as his wife wasn't well enough to travel. While he didn't hear so well, his mind was sharp, and he picked up the new verb tenses faster than I did.

When the class partnered off for dialogue practice, I quickly chose Peter. These kids wouldn't appreciate his stories the way I knew I would! He told me he was a professor of physics and mathematics, and once he found out I was from Salt Lake City, he told me that he and his wife visited my home city a mere half-century ago. Despite the decades since then, he related to me everything he saw (including the Mormon Tabernacle Choir) and how difficult it was to get a cup of tea or coffee!

The teacher assigned topics for us to discuss with our partner, so we moved to the subjects listed and did our best to dialogue in Italian. I laughed out loud when Peter told me the last movie he saw in a theater was *The Sound of Music*!

"It's all been downhill since then," I told him, mixing Italian, English, and charades into the story.

His first love was an older woman who had jilted his brother (when was the last time you heard someone say *jilted*?), and that sly Peter had moved right in! We made a plan to meet for coffee before class the next day, and I knew I was fortunate to have grabbed the seat next to this brilliant, courageous man who continued to learn just for the sake of learning.

I knew full well that I needed more time in language school, but when the course ended, I didn't re-up. I could speak enough Italian to get by, and I wanted to practice in daily conversations with locals when I shopped for vegetables or asked for directions. I could get myself on the right train, find the conductor and explain why I forgot to validate my train ticket, and order in a restaurant. I was eager to spend mornings exploring my city and take day trips to neighboring towns. So, I justified my lack of continuing classes with the fact that I was never going to be an interpreter for the U.N. and opted for more time exploring my new country.

I continued to take any and all tours offered by Alexandra Lawrence, but now she had become a good friend as well as my favorite Florentine guide. As it usually goes, I can't remember the exact moment when we moved from business acquaintances to friends, as the seamless progression made me feel that I had always known her.

Alexandra was an American who has been in Italy since her college days and was married to an Italian. Having received her master's degree in Dante and Italian literature, she was an authority on the history, art, and literature of Florence. Her natural ability to tell a story was what kept her booked months in advance during the busy tourist season.

Alexandra could hold a group of unruly expats like us spellbound while she guided us through the lesser-known attractions of Florence. She had so successfully woven herself into the Florentine community that I always met someone new when I hung out with her.

Today we met at a restaurant called La Bussola on via Porta Rossa. This was one of the few places where truly great pizza was served for lunch, and the waiters were as friendly as they were handsome.

As we looked over the menu, Alexandra looked up. "You're not one of those American girls who can't eat a whole pizza, are you?"

"Of course not," I replied.

I had happily learned that Italians didn't share food and didn't take leftovers home, and I adapted to drinking wine with lunch and eating a whole pizza. Both were made even better by the company of someone with whom I could be completely myself and who understood both the American and Italian sides of my life.

Walking home, I decided to take the long way and walk along the Arno, past the American consulate building and back up on the Oltrarno side. Even though I made this walk several times a week, it never failed to fill my soul with gratitude and a disbelief that I was living here. I breathed in the air of Florence, the sights and sounds that surrounded me, and I breathed in the grace that brought me to this city.

I stopped on Ponte Santa Trinita and looked up toward Ponte Vecchio and to the west where the sun was slipping between two clouds. "What am I supposed to do here?" I said in a whisper.

There was an undercurrent to my walks now, a feeling like I used to sense before a late summer's thunderstorm would break loose and drench the Salt Lake Valley. I could feel something was coming, something was being prepared for me to take hold of, but I hadn't a clue what it was.

I thought, initially, that I would spend time in Florence, heal, and find my joy again. But now, it seemed to be just the first step—with more on the way. Whatever it was, I was open to it. I had learned to surrender to what life offered me and not hold so tightly to the reins.

As I contemplated this and turned to walk home, I looked down at my right hand resting on the bridge. Next to it was a single white feather.

Sixteen

Lord, make me an instrument of Your peace. Where there is hatred, let me sow love; where there is injury, pardon; where there is doubt, faith; where there is despair, hope; where there is darkness, light; where there is sadness, joy. O, Divine Master, grant that I may not so much seek to be consoled as to console; to be understood as to understand; to be loved as to love; for it is in giving that we receive; it is in pardoning that we are pardoned; it is in dying that we are born again to eternal life.

—Saint Francis of Assisi

Nancy and I caught an early train to Assisi one morning. It was about a three-hour trip, and we decided to stay at a bed and breakfast we found online so we could spend an entire day or more in the town.

Walking to the Stazione di Santa Maria Novella, the local train station, was generally about a ten-minute walk. However, at this time of day, it was a bit like salmon swimming upstream. The street was filled with people arriving for their day's work, with a quick stop at a bar for espresso and a pastry. I navigated with my overnight bag as Nancy and I traveled light.

I had already been to Assisi once, and I so loved the prayer of Saint Francis. It was often my morning meditation, and I had been eager to see his hometown and the basilica built to honor him.

Fortunately, I had already been to Assisi and returned when I found out that the Prayer of Saint Francis may not have been written by him. It was a little like hearing about the myth of Santa Claus, but because I had visited Assisi, it didn't matter much. Just as the spirit of Christmas remains, the gentle spirit of Saint Francis permeated his hometown.

The story of Saint Francis is one of a young soldier lost in the ways of the world for much of his life, when he had a vision to serve God. Giving up all of his material possessions, he served with such gentleness and kindness that people were transformed merely by his presence, and animals were drawn to him, unafraid.

While I don't equate my donating thirty-seven pairs of designer shoes to be on par with Saint Francis, I have learned a thing or two about living more simply in the past year. I, too, am traveling much lighter these days.

I also had come to understand that the only way to embrace my new life was to open my heart to a culture and a people very different from my own. And the key to all of it seemed to rest in kindness.

Lord, make me an instrument of Your peace. Where there is hatred, let me sow love...

Nancy and I arrived at the station in Assisi, where we were greeted by our hostess, Mariella, who took our luggage as we bought our tickets to take the bus up the hill to the small town. The winding path before us was decorated with beautiful red and white roses on both sides the road. This morning, the bus was packed, and Nancy and I held on to the hanging straps, trying to maintain our balance and not take anyone out with the purses hanging from our arms.

I watched as Nancy approached a group of four teenage Italian boys, seated close to her. I knew she didn't speak Italian, so I carefully moved over to hear what she was saying.

She asked the young man closest to her to give her his seat, that doing so would make his mother proud! I chuckled under my breath as I delighted in watching her make this happen. The young man's friends were giving him a hard time, and they were all laughing as Nancy took the now-vacant seat in the middle of the boy's three friends.

Nancy was a retired school teacher who had chosen a different country to live in each year. To say that she was gutsy would be an understatement, as these Italian boys had just found out. But Italian mommas are not shy, and I have no doubt that young man knew his mom would have done the same as Nancy.

Brava, sister!

The Basilica Papale di San Francesco stood high on a hill, called "Hill of Paradise," and could be seen from a great distance. Inside the church, the walls were frescoed from top to bottom by the leading artists of the day. Giotto, Cimabue, Simone Martini, and Lorenzetti all helped create a most exquisite monument to the gentle saint from Assisi.

The church was finished in 1243 and was divided into three sections consisting of the saint's tomb, the lower basilica, and the upper basilica. Nancy and I milled around the outside for a few minutes, looking for a place to pay. Finally, we asked a priest and were informed that it was free to enter. *Free?*

Entering the lower basilica, my eyes took a moment to adjust. It was dark; the skilled artists knew their paintings would be seen in this way. The nave was frescoed with parallel scenes from the life of Christ and the life of Saint Francis, all under a brilliant ceiling of stars.

In the upper basilica, light radiated through the windows and the painting from floor to ceiling almost looked like wallpaper to me. As I stood by the podium and gazed up toward the rose-colored stained glass, I gasped a little. It was simply stunning!

I walked down to the lowest level of the basilica, where the saint was buried, and I knew why this was a pilgrimage made by over four million visitors a year. There was a peace and sweetness there inside the small chapel. I walked around the crypt and saw the notes and candles placed there. An old woman knelt in prayer with her hand clasped upon the grate of the crypt. I was moved, and I could see that Nancy was as well.

I remember Dr. Wayne Dyer recalling his experience speaking at the Basilica of Saint Francis. In his forty years of sharing wisdom in a public setting, he called it his most memorable moment. Frozen, unable to speak, he began to sob as he witnessed the spirit of the holy place. I felt honored to be there and knelt in my own prayer of thanksgiving. *Where there is despair, let me bring hope. Where there is darkness, only light.*

The feeling in the basilica seemed to spill over into the small town of Assisi. It was a welcome relief from the bustle and crowds of Florence. Nancy and I wandered through the cobbled streets and checked out the restaurants and the churches of Saint Clare, Chiesa Nuova, and the tiny Saint Stefano.

I stopped in front of a gift store, drawn in to look at lavender sachets shaped like Franciscan monks. Upon entering the store, I found that the entire shop was devoted to all things lavender—soaps, sachets, and body lotions all created in the heavenly scent!

As we walked the narrow and winding streets, we saw many shops selling Umbrian linen: scarves, shirts, table linens, and towels—all of marvelous fabric. Nancy and I both bought a couple of scarves for spring. Even when traveling lightly, a girl still has needs!

Our stroll continued through a chocolate shop with an alcove garden, a *trattoria* for lunch, and several art galleries. On one particularly steep hill, Nancy and I were huffing and puffing as we passed two women, easily in their eighties. I'd seen them walking ahead of us without any difficulty, so I jokingly asked them, "*Dove si trova una palestra*?" (Where would one find a gym?)

They understood the joke, laughed, and answered, "*È qui!*" (It is here!)

It's no wonder the people there live such long lives. The sense of community, where everyone gets dressed for the day and gets out, is huge! But the walking and fresh food has to be part of the equation. Italians are among the healthiest people in the world.

Heading back toward the bus stop, Nancy and I both stopped to admire paintings in the window of a small studio. We stepped inside and were greeted by a handsome Italian man who introduced himself as the artist. He showed us a half-finished piece he was working on. He didn't speak much English and seemed to enjoy my speaking a little Italian.

I told him we lived in Florence, and he asked for my phone number, as he was coming to Florence the next week for business. I hesitated a little but wrote it down for him before I changed my mind. Italian men are so direct, and it always took me back a bit! But, despite a little blushing, I enjoyed the chat.

By the time we reached the bus to head down the hill, we were exhausted and relieved that, this time, there were seats for both of us!

Our hosts had our rooms ready, which were on the second level. It felt very much like we were staying at Grandma and Grandpa's house, complete with cookies and oversized down comforters waiting on our beds.

I awoke in the night and tiptoed to the bathroom next to my bedroom. Directly out the small window, the majestic basilica on the hill caught my eye. Looming over the valley, the walls reflected light to all below, and I paused to take it in. The hush of the darkness had me again in awe—not just of the massive fortress of the basilica, but of the peacefulness it exuded.

The next morning, Mariella's husband, Paul, who was in charge of breakfast, was making our coffee and seeing to it that we had fresh pastries and fruit. I apologized to Paul as he delivered my first cup of coffee and explained that it took copious amounts of hot caffeine to get this girl moving. I don't think he believed me, but as he brought me my third cup in five minutes, he was getting the idea!

Both he and Mariella were gracious and warm, wanting to be certain that we had maps and a plan for the morning. We wanted to see the Basilica of Santa Maria degli Angeli, Saint

Mary of the Angels, which was within walking distance. The basilica was built around the ninth-century Porziuncola, a little church still considered the most sacred place for Franciscans.

Outside, the skies looked a bit dark, and I was happy we would be leaving Assisi by noon. The church was stunning, and we stopped in our tracks as the sound of monks chanting filled the large area surrounding the smaller church where they were seated. We peered inside and saw that there was only room for about eight monks, but their voices filled the space with an overwhelming and ethereal sound.

It was pouring rain by the time we left the church, and neither of us had an umbrella. We stood for a minute under the protection of the overhead portico and pondered our options but concluded we had none! We needed to get back to Mariella and Paul's, get our luggage, and dash to the station to catch our train. Because we were just planning one night's stay, neither of us had a change of pants or shoes. We delayed as long as we could but finally made a run for it.

We ducked under storefronts as we went along in an effort to not be completely soaked, but it was useless. There comes a point in degrees of wetness, and we reached the saturation point! Soaked through our underwear, we were sopping wet.

Mariella and Paul said not to worry as we dripped in the entry way of their bed & breakfast. Mariella wanted to bring us a hair dryer to help, but I wasn't convinced that dry hair would make me any warmer. Italians have real concern over wet hair outside, but we decided to just push our luck and take trash bags to sit on so as not to ruin Mariella's car seats.

Nancy and I looked up and laughed as we sat across from each other like two drowned cats on the train. I've learned if one is overly worried about looking foolish, one should not move to a foreign country! We concluded this would be embarrassing in any country, and my usual pride in packing light was taking a hit.

Somewhere between Arezzo and the Campo di Marte train station, Nancy and I discovered we were almost dry. It was a cold ride back, but nothing could take the joy out of seeing Assisi. Whether in sacred sanctuaries or with a handsome artist in his gallery, people who smiled filled that town.

Later that night, in reading about Saint Francis, I found a quote, which was directly from his writings: "Preach the Gospel at all times, and when necessary, use words."

Seventeen

They began at seven a.m. Even in my deep sleep, I recognized the cadence, the pause, and the full lilt of the morning song of the bells from the campanile of Santa Maria del Fiore, the Duomo di Firenze. And I smiled, while half asleep, because a new day was beginning, and I was home. I was waking up in Florence, Italy—and it felt like I was home.

I started each day with the affirmation that I was home in Florence, because Florence was my home now. I again began counting the days down until I had to leave for Utah, but with a sense of purpose. The purpose would be to obtain a visa and, subsequently, a *Permesso di soggiorno*, and then return here. I needed to apply for a visa from the United States, and although the process was daunting, I was eager to start.

The expat network of ladies was growing, and one day a large group of us met at a restaurant called 4 Leoni for lunch. It was on the Oltrarno side of the Arno, and I was happy to get there, where the crowds are fewer. Since Easter, every week tourist numbers seemed to double, and I found myself, a tourist, feeling very annoyed at sharing my city with so many others.

At lunch I was seated next to Angie Horner, a petite blonde woman who I had not met before. She told me that she and her husband were here for a year and recently wrapped up the *permesso* work. Angie was delightful, and we planned to get together the following week for coffee. She and Doug lived in the San Niccolò neighborhood, and she offered to show me their apartment where we could chat with Doug about the *permesso* guidelines.

I was again struck with how open and generous the expat community was with each other. I realized how little I had had to reach out and make new friends in my life. There was acceptance and welcoming in the group that spoke to our need for community. While I had relied on the kindness of Italians, there was a familiar ease to meeting and becoming friends with other Americans.

Before I met in person Angie's husband, Doug, he sent me an email outlining, in detail, the process for a visa and *permesso*. If there was one quality that Doug possessed even more than generosity, it was detail! He saved me weeks, maybe months, of hair-pulling aggravation and time by sharing his knowledge.

Doug and Angie were the type of people everyone hoped to have in the community. They were a rock-solid couple who both decided to retire from their jobs and take this year off, together, to explore Italy.

One early spring night, I had drinks on Doug and Angie's small but inviting terrace neighboring the Bardini Garden with a clear sky overhead. I, once again, felt like I had won the lottery to be seated among my new friends and was optimistic that night that I truly could make a life here, which meant living in Italy legally.

Doug and Angie told me they were moving from the city of Florence for the summer months to a small town, Impruneta, which was about eighteen kilometers away. They met their landlords, Donatella and Andrea, who would be living in the apartment under theirs, and as they described the views of the countryside, I was eager to visit! Doug had an old car shipped to Italy, so they would be able to drive back and forth from Florence. It sounded idyllic, but I realized without a car, and living *da sola* (alone), it could be quite isolating for me.

Learning to be alone was a new experience for me and not an altogether comfortable one. Knowing that there were insights

I could only experience through spending time in meditation and solitude, I had, as Pema Chödrön encourages, been leaning into the discomfort.

It's an interesting sensation when a thought or memory is painful, to stay with it rather than mentally run. I'd spent so much of my life surrounded by friends, children, partners, students, clients, and loud music, that I hadn't spent a lot of time just being still. Now, I found silence becoming a welcome companion, and I made friends with myself in a new way. Just as I drew up a map for the new day, I tried to map out and guide myself through loneliness. I knew there were lessons in it for me, and the gift would be in knowing what they were.

I resisted letting my thoughts run too far ahead to a place where I tried to figure out what was around the next corner in my life. Quietly, I accepted my past and focused on staying in the present. I was even trying to accept that if I was unable to get a visa, somehow it would be okay; there would be a different plan. So far, that line of thought was not sitting well with me!

I was still making a weekly trek up to San Miniato to challenge my aerobic capacity as well as to say a prayer once inside the church. My lungs seemed to have adapted to the task as well as the altitude change. Evidence that my prayers were being answered appeared every day, as I was meeting remarkable people who stepped into my life just as I needed them.

Climbing the steps one day, my iPod offered Melissa Etheridge's *Talking to My Angel*, the song that was played at the end of the funeral of my dear friend Amy Stewart. "I can feel the thunder underneath my feet. I sold my soul for freedom. It's lonely but it's sweet."

I felt Amy jog beside me as my legs burned on the last flight of stairs. I did feel the thunder under my feet, although I didn't know where it was coming from. I could sense its approach, however, as surely as I could feel Amy cheering me on from another realm. I was not afraid. I'd been talking to my angel, and she said that it's all right.

Eighteen

I think I went to Italy initially for the art, architecture, food, and history. But I stayed there because of the people of Cortona.

—Frances Mayes

May in Florence was sun-and-tourist-drenched. I found my city more and more crowded and was looking for a new town to visit whenever I could find someone to travel with me. The smaller cities around Florence were less crowded, and in the back of my mind was always the thought that if I didn't get a visa, I may not get back here. It drove me to maximize the time I had to travel, just in case.

The Pollyanna in me said I would return, but I learned enough about life to know that nothing is a given, and plans can veer off in directions we never see coming. I checked off so many towns and cities from my list, especially those that could be done in a day trip. There seemed to always be one or more of our group who wanted to jump on a train and head off to an adventure.

When the group met for *aperitivo* one night, the conversation turned to Cortona. Seemed everyone had visited there but me, and with just a few weeks left in Florence, I was eager to plan a trip to this hill town. Between tours, classes, and workshops, everyone else was committed for the upcoming weekend, but I was determined to see this spot made famous by Frances Mayes in her popular book and movie *Under the Tuscan Sun*.

I generally would leave early in the morning for a new city and return late at night to avoid paying for a hotel room (and I had grown fond of my Murphy bed). But, since this might have been my only chance to visit, I decided to stay overnight in Cortona. In researching on Google, I selected a not-so-expensive hotel, made a reservation, and read up on this ancient Etruscan town.

On the train, I strained to hear the announcements and looked out the filthy windows so as not to miss my stop. Cortona is eighty-two minutes from Florence and rests high on a hill. I had learned that the train stopped at Camucia, the town below. I had no idea how far away Camucia was from Cortona, but I had called the hotel, and they said they would send someone to pick me up at the station.

When I arrived in Camucia, I was a bit taken aback by how small it is. There was only one other person getting off the train there, and there was no bar, restroom, or ticket counter. I made my way through the empty room that served as the station and out to the front, wondering what I had committed myself to for two days.

There were a few parked cars and a couple of men standing around, but otherwise, no activity. I called the hotel to tell them I had arrived.

"*Si, si, Signora. Mariano arriva presto,*" the woman on the other end of the call told me.

Mariano's shift at the hotel had apparently ended when he received the call to drive me up the hill. It was not a hotel shuttle bus but a small, gray compact car with a dent in the back door that arrived to pick me up. The man who stepped out had jet-black hair and brusquely said hello. Mariano introduced himself as he opened the passenger-side door for me but first had to move his jacket and stacks of paper so I could get inside.

"You work for the hotel?" I asked him.

"Yes, of course," he replied in English, with very little accent and no smile.

I was still cautiously standing outside the car, even though Mariano had loaded my overnight bag into the trunk. I was thinking it was not an altogether smart thing to climb into a stranger's car (isn't that what I always told my children?) in a town where I didn't know a soul.

Mariano shrugged his shoulders with his palms turned up. It was the classic Italian pose meaning, "What?" I decided I had no choice but to trust him. I shifted and sized him up again and noticed a slight smile as he got behind the wheel.

I climbed inside and started speaking in Italian, hoping to convince him I was not as green as I appeared. He was laughing now and told me that he spoke better English *and* German than I spoke Italian, so let's switch to English. I couldn't argue with that, even if I was a little insulted!

As we climbed the hill to Cortona, Mariano chuckled at my barrage of questions. The height provided me with a view of the countryside, Lake Trasimeno, and the town above us. I asked Mariano about the church I saw high on the hill and the others we passed by. I couldn't stand not to take it all in, so I undid my seat belt to turn completely around in my seat, perched on my knees.

Mariano informed me I needed to sit back down but asked me if I would like it if he took me on a tour later in the day. I hesitated. I wanted a tour, especially by a local, but was it smart to go off alone with someone I didn't know? I told him yes, and we arranged a time and a price, which made it seem like a business venture and nothing more. I figured I could ask the lady at the front desk of the hotel about Mariano's character.

I had only a half-hour to check in and get to my room for a quick wash-up before I went out again, but I was so eager to see more of Cortona. Checking in and talking with the front desk lady, I was assured that I was in good hands with Mariano and had nothing to fear. I took the elevator to my floor and checked into a room that was small but clean, with time just to drop my luggage on the bed.

Mariano was waiting for me in Piazza Garibaldi, a circular area for cars, people, and a few benches. The overlook was amazing, views that went on forever, and there were more people there than I anticipated.

I had told Mariano on the drive up from the station that I wanted to see Bramasole, where Frances from *Under the Tuscan Sun* had lived. He didn't seem too impressed.

"That's not really the most important landmark of Cortona," he said with a bit of a disapproving tone.

"So, what *is* an important landmark in Cortona?" I asked my guide.

"I'll make you a deal, *cara*," Mariano said, using the term of endearment. "I'll take you to see Bramasole, but first we will go to Le Celle and the church of Santa Margherita." Who was I to argue?

Mariano drove us outside the city walls of Cortona and back through a wooded, one-lane road. Again, the views were breathtaking—so much so I forgot to be nervous about Mariano at all.

As we headed down the road, Mariano pulled over for another car to get by and for a monk who was walking along the roadside. Mariano explained to me that Le Celle was still home to six monks, but at one time there were many more. They were the followers of Saint Francis, who came to live in this remote location when he had needed a place for retreat from Assisi—a quiet, reflective spot where he could meditate and pray. The land was donated to him for his sanctuary in 1211 A.D., and a structure of nine cells was built. Saint Francis stayed in the remote sanctuary often, once for a period of two years.

As Mariano gave me the history of Le Celle, I was moved at the synchronicity which had led me here. Already feeling a deep connection to Saint Francis, I had no idea that he had ever left Assisi, but I wanted to know more.

Mariano assured me that most people, even Italians, didn't know about Le Celle. Still, he was giving me a bit of a reprove, albeit kindly, for coming to Cortona to see Bramasole but not Le Celle.

Mariano parked the small, gray car in a lot with a couple of other cars already there. He walked me to the entrance and read the wooden sign that was written in Italian. It welcomed those who came to visit but asked all who enter to do so prayerfully, that the spirit of Saint Francis remains in this sanctuary.

I had no preconceived idea of what Le Celle would look like, but I was speechless. Built into the side of the mountain is a group of cells and a monastery, surrounded by trees. I felt a gentle breeze in the warm air, heard the birds singing, but there was a silent peacefulness there that I had not felt before, even inside a church.

Mariano told me to take all the time I wanted to, but I was to explore Le Celle on my own. He said he would wait for me in the parking lot. He pointed to a path that led through the dense trees and told me to follow that way back to the car.

A long, sloping path led down to a running creek and, crossing the bridge, I saw and heard the waterfall. There was vegetation all around me, gorgeous flowering plants of pinks and yellows, and a vegetable garden, but not another soul in sight.

Not knowing where to go exactly, I took the steps on my right and entered a small, dark room with a prayer bench, flowers, and a sign pointing to the cell of Saint Francis. Three more steps up, I looked into the tiny enclosure where the beloved saint slept. I was overcome with emotion. As I walked toward the prayer bench, I was grateful for it, as my legs felt wobbly and unsure.

I knelt inside the rock walls of this sacred space and offered the only prayer I knew—a prayer of gratitude. My heart overflowed with the wonder I felt at being there, so far removed from my home and all I was used to, to kneel where a saint had knelt before me and offer a prayer in the space where he offered so many. I recognized again in this moment the gift that this time and place had given me—to grow and to learn about what made my heart sing. Most of all, my time in Italy had helped me find my joy again.

Wiping my tears, I walked through another door and out into the bright, sunlit patio that overlooked the stream. I paused to take in the view, now looking up to the entrance of Le Celle with rock walls and arched bridges. Mariano was wise to let me explore this on my own, and while I had no idea which way I was supposed to go, I enjoyed the solitary exploration.

I turned and walked up a flight of stairs that was enclosed by cool cement walls with a small opening for a window. At the top I looked down to see a small, white feather resting on the tip of my boot.

"Yes," I said out loud to my angels. "This is certainly something I was supposed to see."

I huffed and puffed up the slope to the back side of the parking lot and was rewarded with a view of Cortona in the distance, its ancient walls surrounding the city and a church at the edge of town. I imagined Saint Francis taking in this view. I saw Mariano standing by the car smoking and watching me as I walked toward him.

"So, what does the American lady think of Cortona now?" he asked, somewhat smugly.

I had no words, and my eyes were still filled with tears.

"Yes," he said, softening, "and you thought you were coming to Cortona just to visit Bramasole."

Mariano and I returned to the hotel, and I looked in my purse to find some cash. He had taken me to the church high above the town where Santa Margherita lay inside a glass case—a feature he neglected to warn me about. He also, begrudgingly, took me to see Bramasole—that looked just like it did in the movie!

I was touched by Mariano's kindness and his desire to reveal to me the true jewels outside the city walls of Cortona. He was proud of his town and generously shared his knowledge with me.

As we finished the tour, Mariano asked me where I planned to eat dinner. Again, I hesitated just a bit. Was he asking me out to dinner or just checking on my plans? I assured him I had a couple of places in mind and had done my research and asked some friends, to which he shook his head and laughed under his breath.

"No, you haven't," he said, "and they won't tell you where to go for an authentic Italian dinner anyway. This is why you need me."

Okay. I was busted. I acquiesced and asked him where I should go for dinner.

"You go to *La Grotta*, and you tell Guido that I sent you."

I was finished being skeptical of Mariano, as he hadn't led me astray yet. In fact, he'd been an absolute gift. I assured him I would find *La Grotta* and Guido at dinnertime.

Back in my room, I was thinking to unpack and have a shower before going back out. The room was dark, and the shutters were heavy green, typical Tuscan-styled coverings, which can bar the sun from entering a room even in the daylight hours. I pulled back the lock and opened them to find not only a view but a small terrace outside.

I pushed the windows open and stepped out onto the small enclosed area, just big enough to stand on and take in the view across the valley. Over the terracotta rooftops, I had a view that I thought only existed in postcards! I was tucked into the hills, and the entire valley below me was spread out like a patchwork quilt with occasional wisps of smoke coming from the farm lands. Off to the left, I saw the lake Mariano told me separates Tuscany from its neighboring region of Umbria. I breathed in the air and took in the view and this day.

It started as a slow rumble much like I remembered from my days in a Utah earthquake. I felt a sensation that began in my toes, moved up to my solar plexus, and climbed to settle in my heart. My head was swimming, but my understanding was crystal clear. I knew what I was supposed to do in Tuscany!

The adrenaline rush surged through my entire body, and I remembered this same sense of certainty from the coffee shop in Rome where I made the decision to move here. A plan was shown to me as clearly as I saw the warm valley below. I knew what the next step was! My excitement was about to spill over, but there was a calm undercurrent keeping me still.

I was destined to share Tuscany with other women! I would assist them in finding their own sense of joy and beauty here. I didn't know yet how that would unfold, but I knew I would make it happen. I felt it with every breath I took; this is what I was to do. The same force that helped me find my inner peace and passion showed me my next step.

I had walked up and down the Arno River for months asking the skies for an answer, and I found it here in Cortona, just two weeks before I was to return to the U.S.!

I was euphoric but centered and certain. I laughed and danced on the small terrace when I realized how simple the answer was! I didn't know the cursed "hows" yet, but I knew it would happen. I would create a tour company for women and share with them the beauty of Tuscany.

After a quick shower, I dressed for dinner in Cortona and ventured out. At the corner of via Nazionale, I wandered slowly and gazed into each store. When I came to the main piazza, I saw the local townspeople gathering together for *aperitivo*. The street was lined with tables and chairs, checkered tablecloths, and lively conversation.

The benches facing inward on Piazza della Repubblica were all occupied by men, and I guessed the average age to be about ninety-two. I watched them as they watched their square—probably the same view they had had each evening for decades. Unlike the high-fashion, fast-paced Florentines, these locals seemed to be typical of small-town Tuscany.

Clearly, everyone knew everybody else in this tiny community, and the greetings rang out down via Nazionale and throughout the piazza. Small children raced up and down the stairs of the city hall, and the feeling was relaxed and congenial. I wondered, as I lingered by the flower shop, if a woman ever dared to take a seat with the fraternal group on the benches. I had the sense that I was watching a movie, and the scene was unfolding just on my behalf. I was thoroughly enchanted by this place, and only my growling stomach made me turn to find the *trattoria* Mariano suggested.

Down a short alley was the sign for *La Grotta*. When I entered, I wondered if perhaps I came in a back way or even into the kitchen entrance. I was greeted in Italian by a smiling gentleman, and I asked him in my stammering Italian if he was Guido, and was there a table for me, slipping in that I was a friend of Mariano's.

"*Certo, certo, Signora, ma da sola?*" Guido said a bit sadly, asking me if I was eating alone.

Ah, yes, apparently in Cortona they would worry about me as well! Being alone and eating alone in Italy is a bit of a mystery to most Italians, and they are dreadfully afraid one feels sad about their solo experience.

I smiled and told him it was just me as I looked around the small entry again and into the kitchen. Still uncertain as to whether I entered the wrong way, I saw that Guido had taken off, and I was to follow. We entered a small room with an arched ceiling and rock walls. I felt like we were in a cave, with seven small tables. Guido took me through another arched doorway into an even smaller room where four tables were set with cheerful pink linen and dishes.

Even though it was obvious my Italian was limited, Guido spoke no English and was rattling off the daily specials and a litany of information that flew over my head. I ordered water and wine and sat back to look over the menu.

Any sense of feeling uncomfortable about dining alone vanished when my meal arrived. I had taken Guido's recommendation, and the ravioli stuffed with ricotta, topped with pine nuts, fresh basil, and tomatoes may have been the best thing I had ever eaten! While I sipped on my wine after dinner, Guido insisted I have dessert.

Resistance is futile, especially when it's about dessert, and the tiramisu was exquisite. I was beyond full, beyond happy, and beyond in love with this new town I discovered.

I might have also been just a bit tipsy, so rather than walk around the town, as I had planned, I returned to my hotel room. I wanted some time to digest dinner—*and* my day. I had made a decision, and it was one that would take me off in a new direction. I wanted to think about Le Celle, and Santa Margherita, and how it was that a new friend named Mariano appeared at the perfect time to show me these experiences.

One of the most common questions I get from Americans is whether I have seen the movie *Under the Tuscan Sun*. Most are certain that was where I got the idea to head off to Tuscany and begin a new life! But I had never read the book and vaguely remembered the movie. That night I was interested to see what caused people to draw the parallels from my life to the movie and also to see the movie's backdrop of Cortona.

I downloaded the movie on my computer and curled up on the bed. I guess something happened after the opening credits, but I didn't see it. Sometime in the night I shut down the computer and climbed inside the covers.

Nineteen

My suitcase was opened on my bed, and the sorting/tossing/packing process had begun. I mumbled under my breath something to the effect that we should all just get to live wherever we want to, as I assessed my clothing and its worthiness to travel across the ocean with me. I had to exit Italy for ninety days, as I didn't have a visa yet, and I was not happy to be going.

The inexplicably high pile of scarves seemed to mock me. I wouldn't need those in the summer months in Utah.

Delta Airlines said bags had to weigh fifty pounds or less, but my real concern with their weight was whether I could navigate the airport alone with them. While I had lived small those past three months, Italian fashion is dangerous, and I succumbed to more shoes and sweaters than I had planned on purchasing.

Lorenzo offered to store a suitcase in Florence for me, but I felt a little guilty asking him to do so. I decided to rent from an agency that specialized in helping Americans through the *Permesso di soggiorno* process, including rental contracts, and so I hesitated to ask him for a favor. He assured me he understood my decision to rent from someone else, that he knew nothing about obtaining a *permesso*, and assured me I would be in good hands with this new agent. I promised him I'd come to visit as soon as I returned.

With the new agency I located an apartment overlooking the Bardini Garden in the San Niccolò area. It seemed to be perfect, with the exception of the fifty-six steps up; no elevator.

I loved the area, which was less crowded and more of a local's neighborhood, but I hated leaving Lorenzo and his watchful care over me.

It was only the first part of June, but the heat and humidity in Italy were oppressive. There was very little air-conditioning in apartments or businesses, and I looked forward to the American lifestyle of temperature control. I also looked forward to not worrying if I wanted to dry my hair while the washing machine was running.

But when in Utah, I missed so much on the other side of the ocean.

I missed the slower pace of dining in Italy, the emphasis on enjoying the experience with friends, good food, and conversation. I missed the mental stimulation of tours and classes on subjects I never studied before. I missed the sounds of Florence with its international languages, blaring opera, lively soccer games, and the bells, all melding into a blissful cacophony that was the daily rhythm of my life.

I wouldn't miss the post office.

I closed and zipped my suitcases and, standing on the bed, lifted them one at a time to determine their weight. I'd become pretty accurate with this less-than-scientific method!

I stored them in the corner and closed up the Murphy bed to do some stretching on the colorfully designed rug. Deeply I inhaled my gratitude, slowly I exhaled in surrender. I had lived the past year in the present moment, not necessarily because I became more enlightened, but because I had no choice. I really had not known what was coming up next, and surrendering to that had been a lesson in trust.

My body was flowing through the yoga pose Sun Salutation, and I felt its gratitude as I stretched the tight muscles at the back of my legs. My face was just inches off the floor as I blankly studied the colors and pattern swirls of blue and red in the rug.

My mind flashed involuntarily back to a time, just over a year ago when, collapsed on the floor of my basement, when I stared at another piece of carpet. Thomas had grabbed my right arm when I had placed a hand on his chest, asking him not to leave during an argument.

In a split second, with his martial arts training, he had my arm in a spiral twist. The pain was excruciating, and I fell to my knees, begging him to release me. His expression made me realize that this was a man I had never really known. He was telling me that he had the power to break my arm with one more twist if I didn't stay out of his way, and I had no doubt that he would. Finally dropping me, he flew up the stairs and out the door. I stayed in a heap on the floor and stared at the carpet.

In the minutes that followed, I memorized the varying colors of the shag carpet, the slight fuzz on each strand, the still-new smell it had.

I was numb. I was where so many other women had been: in shock that the man I gave my love to could use his superior physical strength to harm me. I was confused, but I got up, walked up the stairs and assessed my injury. And then I took pictures.

The pealing of the bells from around Florence brought me back to the present moment, and I finished stretching and moved up off the floor. I pulled on my trusty walking shoes, headed on out the door to be among the sights and sounds of my present-day world, and let the sting of the past fade from my thoughts.

Walking across Piazza della Signoria with a slice of pizza from Pizzeria Toto was the perfect cure for whatever ailed me just then. Strains of guitar music floated in the air as I strolled around the open-air loggia, admired the statues, and finished my pizza.

I was not the same woman I was a year ago; I knew that much was true. The woman who had stood in the small coffee shop in Rome may have had a glimmer this one existed, but she had a lot of steps to take first. I had learned that to live my own truth had disappointed some people, but I had come to know there was no other choice for me.

Twenty

I stood in the darkness on via Calzaiuoli at four-thirty in the morning, wishing I could bypass the next twenty hours and just beam myself to Salt Lake City. I knew what this day would bring—a long haul. I tried to focus on the fact that before the day ended I would see Justin and Lauren.

I heard singing a few streets over. The loud, slurred voices and laughter of young kids who'd undoubtedly been out all night faded into the near dawn. I tried not to think about leaving Florence. The thought of not being here in the morning, waking to the bells, made my eyes sting with tears. Now, tucked away in my suitcase was the folder containing all the rental documents I would need to apply for a visa from the Italian consulate in the U.S. That would be my main project for the next three months.

I tried to visualize the Wasatch Mountain range and the Salt Lake Valley. That valley had been my home and home to four generations before me. Its rugged granite walls were the backdrop of my childhood and later for my children.

I thought about large diet colas filled with crunchy ice, celebrating my upcoming birthday with the Dodo girls, shopping at Banana Republic, and eating Indian food. I tried to think of what I loved about being in the U.S.—washing and wearing clothes in the same day and Amazon delivering packages!

While I'd be staying with Lauren and sleeping on a futon, I was planning to travel to California to see Sherrilee and to

New Mexico to see Shauna. It would be comforting to be with friends who knew my history and my heart, but it was achingly difficult to describe to them what my days were like now.

I reminded myself it was only for a little while and tried to take comfort in knowing that Florence would be overrun with tourists and the steaming heat soon. But at that moment, in the stillness, Florence seemed like *paradiso*. I looked up at the outline of the Duomo carving out her massive stature against the starlit sky and said a little prayer.

"Please let me come back," I whispered.

Twenty-One

June 2013

For two weeks on either side of the ocean, I was completely upside down on my days and nights. Crashing at seven-thirty in the evening made me not only an unpopular dinner companion but had me wide awake at three a.m. It was futile to resist much, so I didn't as I acclimated to the new time zone.

I prowled the tiny condo and settled into my coffee and morning reading while it was really still nighttime, trying not to wake Lauren. Each week I extended the waking by an hour, but the process never became easier.

My days were filled that June with friends, lunches, and long walks. I didn't feel the push to visit a gym, despite having done so for thirty-two years prior. I had found the pleasure of walking—feeling the earth under my feet, being outside in nature—and the old aches that plagued me during the years I taught fitness classes were now gone.

I had spent hours researching forums and websites for information on successfully acquiring a visa. A few times, I had even placed a call to the Italian consulate's office in San Francisco, only to have a recording tell me the voice mailbox was full. Apparently, even in the U.S., the Italian bureaucracy operated like Italy.

There was, however, an honorary consulate in Salt Lake City, and I decided to go through him, thereby saving the expense of a flight to and hotel in San Francisco. Some on the expat forum I visited had opined that may be a mistake. Many mentioned the benefit of having a face-to-face conversation, and I knew that would help, but I felt like it would be worth a shot to try locally first. A couple of nights, meals, and a flight to San Francisco was a lot of money.

I was worried that as a new honorary consulate, Mr. Homer may not have had a lot of experience with visa applications, but I trusted that he knew the rules better than I did!

In the weeks prior, I had painstakingly collected all the necessary documents and papers needed to prove I was neither a terrorist nor a criminal. I needed to show that I would also not be a burden on the Italian economy by taking a job that could go to an Italian and that I carried my own health insurance. I also needed to provide a copy of my fingerprints and letters from my bank manager and financial advisor that stated I was solvent for at least a year. I'd wondered if they wanted my firstborn as well. Suffice it to say, there were not many of my secrets left once the paperwork was completed.

There's an interesting (frustrating) catch-22 with the application for the visa. I had to show proof that I had purchased a round-trip airline ticket, and the return flight had to be within a ninety-day period after arrival, despite the fact that the reason I was applying for the visa was to stay longer than ninety days. In other words, if my application was successful, the return ticket would be void.

I also had to show a rental contract for a period longer than ninety days, demonstrating that I had a place to live should I be granted a visa. The rental contract had required a hefty deposit, all non-refundable. The process was filled with speed bumps such as these, and I'd decided it was just to weed out those who weren't fully committed, or to find those of us who should be committed—to the loony bin.

Each new document and paper took time, and waiting for appointments slowed that down even more. I was not running out of time but certainly running out of patience wanting to know where my life was going to be lived for the next year.

The morning of my appointment, I was off for a walk through my old neighborhood and then would meet with the honorary consulate in Salt Lake. I left the condo and walked directly up Evergreen Avenue. Immediately, I was transported back to my childhood. The new, modern-looking recreation center had been built where once there was a yellow-brick library. We went as a school class, on a bus, once every two weeks, where I would stock up on books, and dive into a good story, reading in bed with a flashlight under the covers long after bedtime.

This day, I was keenly aware that the streets seemed closer together, and when I passed Gayle Platt's house, I stopped. Gayle was like a sister to me, and as a child I spent as much time at her house as she did at mine. The difference was, at mine we would babysit, and at hers there was a swimming pool and trampoline!

I crossed the street to take a better look at the home I remembered as well as my own. Gayle and I had loved musicals, and we danced and sang our way through our own renditions of them all summer long. Born just eleven days ahead of me, we'd met at her swimming pool when we were five years old and had gone all through school together. I don't remember a significant event of my childhood that she wasn't part of.

I walked close enough to the house to hear the familiar sound of the creek running, and immediately I was transported back to nights under the stars, in sleeping bags, on the trampoline. I had a childhood that was spent in motion, and summers stretched out blissfully in unscheduled hours of riding bikes, building forts, and dancing.

Gayle had been with me on my first trip to Europe in 1972 when we traveled for six weeks with a group of other teenagers through a school program. I had celebrated my seventeenth birthday in Italy, with a liquor-soaked cake that had stung my throat, unaware that I would ever return.

I resisted the urge to knock on the door and ask if I could walk through a stranger's home. I decided I wouldn't want to see the changes anyway. The memories were so sweet, and crystal clear, of my childhood best friend and her home, and I preferred to keep them just as they were.

As I continued up the street, I thought about how love doesn't change. Gayle moved away from Utah when we were twenty-one and never moved back. Yet through all the years, all the children (she had six, I had two), divorce (mine, not hers), heartaches, and triumphs, she had always been just a phone call away. No matter how long the time between our visits, I hear her voice, and I am connected in the deepest sense to my roots—to someone who knows me and my history.

Just a half block away was my childhood home, and my pace picked up with anticipation. I hadn't lived there since I was seventeen, but it was the home of my youth, and I loved seeing it and the neighborhood. The trees had dwarfed the houses, and some of the neighbors had remodeled, but thankfully, mine looked pretty much the same. The upper wooden balcony was still painted an awful green, and seeing the basement door, which provided an easy escape on summer nights, made me smile.

I continued farther up the hill and passed my elementary school. I walked around the building and vividly remembered each classroom, the smell of school lunch, the teachers that often proclaimed me a "good student, but a bit too social." I stopped to take a picture of the spot of my first kiss, with my first boyfriend, Rick. He was still a good friend and probably the nicest man on the planet. It seemed like a lifetime ago.

I dressed up for my appointment with the honorary consulate, as I'd learned from the Italians that it matters! Those women didn't walk out to empty the trash without being fully put together, and I found it shocking how casual Americans were. It wasn't just jeans anymore—Utahns head to the airport in their pajamas!

I met Mike Homer, and we reviewed each sheet of paper that was to be included in the packet for the Italian consulate in San Francisco. It was the consulate, not the honorary consulate, who would make the final decision.

Some of the requirements were tedious, but I had learned a lot from my first year in Italy, one of the biggest lessons being that I'm not in charge. And so, I would happily play by their rules if they would let me stay.

My rental contract was from September 2013 to May 2014, as my plan was to return to Utah for the summer. Everyone had warned me about summers in the Florentine heat and humidity, and I was happy to leave the tourists and the weather for those three months.

Honorary Consulate Homer concluded that it all looked good, and so I added my passport to the packet and turned it over to him to mail.

I was a little concerned with my attachment to this plan. Hadn't this past year been all about letting go? Hadn't I learned to trust that I was being guided each step of the way and to release the need to understand how it would all unfold? I knew that to be too attached was to not surrender, and so, as I walked out of Mr. Homer's office and into the Salt Lake City sunshine, I tried to release any expectations. I had done everything I possibly could to make living full-time in Italy a reality; now I had to let the process work.

There was a gnawing in the pit of my stomach that wouldn't surrender, however. I knew what I was supposed to do in Tuscany, as it was made crystal clear to me looking out the window in Cortona. I knew I was to share this adventure with other women and teach them what I knew of joy and courage. I tried to trust that the Universe would conspire to make it happen.

Twenty-two

Thomas continued to send me emails. He knew that I must have been back in Utah by this point and sent me a birthday greeting asking if we could get together. I deflected the invitation but took a hard look at my own culpability in this never-ending story.

How was it that I hadn't made myself clear and completely severed the relationship months ago? Was it more important to me that I was seen as nice, rather than to stand in my own integrity and decisions?

Here was a man who had never taken responsibility, or even expressed remorse, over physically abusing me. And yet, somehow, he could send me a birthday card and portray himself as the victim.

For the first time since the age of sixteen, I had spent a year not wanting to include a man in my life. While coffee and a dinner date with the artist from Assisi were a nice ego boost, they had finally seemed to be more effort than fun. I was completely enthralled with my new life in Florence and a little afraid that to let someone else in would have meant losing the delight I had found in the adventure.

I knew that the mail was delivered around eleven forty each morning, so I stood by the community mailboxes waiting. I had heard from those who had applied before me that my passport would be returned, and it would either include a visa attached to one of the pages, or not. All the documents and the cost of applying would be gone if the application was denied, but I had made five copies of each as a backup.

The stories of the process taking six weeks had me a little worried, but they were wrong in my case; less than two weeks later, I had a response from the Italian consulate in San Francisco.

Holding the envelope in my hand, I walked back to the condo. I was suddenly nauseated. My entire plans for the next year were hanging in the answer within this envelope and, more than anything, my heart was set on living in Florence.

I walked back to my small bedroom and sat down on the futon. Tearing through the envelope I saw not just my passport, but also a sheet of paper. I opened the paper first and read, *We regret to inform you that your visa application has been denied.*

Why? I had supplied everything that was asked for and had no idea why I had been turned down. I looked down at the sheet of paper again and saw that they included a list of reasons why a visa may be denied, and they had checked the box that said that my time commitment was not long enough.

Disappointment washed over me like a wave. Had I been too hopeful to believe that I could achieve this goal, when so many I knew had not? I went back to the expat forum, which seemed to be the best resource I'd found, and put the question out there.

Had I made a mistake in only arranging a nine-month stay, rather than a year?

Out in the virtual universe, these kind people had led me through many steps of this process, and I quickly received an answer from one of the known authorities. "Yes," he wrote. "The consulate would look at a nine-month stay as a long vacation, and that is not what a visa is for."

I indulged myself in another minute of dismay, and then regrouped. I had to contact my rental agency in Florence and obtain a new contract—this time for a year. Now I was feeling a time crunch, as I was only six weeks away from my scheduled flight back to Florence, and an apartment contract that was to begin on that date.

I compiled all the sheets of paper, called Mr. Homer, and requested a new appointment. After that, I started to think about what to write in a new cover letter.

After some consideration, I decided the best plan was simply to acknowledge in my cover letter that this was my second time applying for a visa in the past six weeks. I included that I had corrected what they checked as the reason for denial, and I hoped there was nothing else lacking in my application.

I had a Skype call with Adriana at the rental agency in Florence and was assured that my new contract would be drawn up and sent. Everything seemed difficult in that when paperwork was sent from another country, communication was harder with the time change and translations.

I'd heard many stories of people who had to apply multiple times for a visa, so I knew this wasn't unusual, but my time in Salt Lake was running out. I wanted to return to Florence, but not just for three months. I wanted to live there!

This time, when I arrived at the honorary consulate's office, it was Mrs. Homer who took me through the process. She went through each piece of paper and weeded out some that were unnecessary. I watched closely as she efficiently stamped each and every page, and she told me that it appeared to all be in good order.

I felt calm and confident, despite my recent denial. Part of my confidence was just defiance, as I hadn't come up with an alternative plan if I didn't get to live in Italy for the next year. I had no house, business, or possessions to speak of in Salt Lake City. I had made my move forward, and now I figured it was the Universe's turn.

On a typical Sunday morning I was seated in my favorite chair, the sun streaming in over my left shoulder as I had coffee time with my girl. I worked on the *New York Times* crossword puzzle, as she occasionally shared with me excerpts from a new blog she was following. I stopped for a moment and took a deep breath in. These were the moments of life to cherish. I knew that these were the good stuff. I'd lived in more luxurious places, for sure, but I'd also learned enough to know that this what fed my soul.

I moved from the puzzle to check my email. I saw one from Thomas. For the past year when I would see an email from him, I'd postpone opening it. It seemed so laborious to wade through, and then I knew I'd have to write a response, which I would dread doing. This time, before I had even known what he had written, I decided, *basta!* Enough!

As I read through the predictable words in his email, I realized his sadness was not even about having lost me. It was about his being lonely, not being in control, and, most of all, his being left. His actions had shown me exactly that for years.

Whenever I had wanted a commitment from him, he had all the excuses why that couldn't happen, the majority of which revolved around his finances. I had allowed him to move in with me for six weeks one winter so he could rent his condo in the warmer climate of Saint George, Utah, and make enough money to pay off his credit card debt. Then, I had hoped, and which he had vaguely agreed to, we could move forward to have a life and a home together.

My response on this Sunday morning in July was quick and to the point. No, I wouldn't be willing to meet and talk. We were not a couple, I was not staying in Utah, and our relationship was long over. I wrote that all of the reasons for that he should fully understand, we'd certainly argued over them enough. And then, I reiterated, just for emphasis, we were done.

With that, I closed my email and got another cup of coffee each for Lauren and me as we relished our lazy Sunday morning.

Twenty-three

I booked a trip to Long Beach, California, for the end of August. I wanted an escape from the Utah heat and to spend some time with my dearest girlfriend, Sherrilee, whose marriage of twenty years had ended the previous December.

While we had Skype calls across the ocean, and she had been in Utah earlier in the summer, nothing compared to just hanging out without a schedule and sharing hours of face-to-face conversation.

Lauren predicted my visa would arrive that Friday, but that didn't keep me from checking the mail every day—sometimes twice. She had Friday off of work, and I think she'd hoped to be with me to share in either the celebration or disappointment.

I rediscovered my childhood fondness for swimming that summer and loved the feel of gliding through the water in the bright sunshine. The pool was right outside of Lauren's condo, and I was usually the only one using it.

One hot afternoon, as I climbed out of the water, I heard my muffled cell phone ringing under the towel that protected it from the heat. I fumbled through the bulky towel, followed the noise, and saw it wasn't a number I recognized, but the caller ID said San Francisco.

I dripped dry as I answered and affirmed my name to a woman who identified herself as being with the Italian consulate. She said she had looked through my application, but I had failed to check the box as to whether I was married, single, divorced, or widowed. I told her I was divorced and paused to see if there was more, but she quickly thanked me and said goodbye.

I sat down on the chaise lounge, felt the hot sun beat down on my back, and tried to think of the implications of the call. Would the Italian consulate's assistant have bothered to call if my application was an obvious *no*? It was hard to imagine standard procedure was to call everyone who failed to check the appropriate marital status box. I wanted to take this omen as a good sign but almost didn't dare.

I decided the only thing I knew for sure was that someone at the consulate's office was reviewing my application, and my answer would be coming soon.

Friday morning at eleven thirty-nine I was at the mailboxes. I'd come to know the mailman's schedule, and this would be the earliest he would have delivered our mail.

I hoped Lauren's intuition was right, that the answer would arrive today. At some point I had decided just knowing would be better than the suspended anxiety.

My hands were shaking as I pulled the now-recognizable envelope from the cool space of the mailbox. I walked quickly back to the condo, opened the door, and called to Lauren, "It's here!"

She joined me in the living room, but I couldn't bring myself to open the letter. It had become too important; it meant too much. I'd waited all summer for this answer, but I felt frozen, and I couldn't seem to rip open the envelope to read the contents.

Initially I asked Lauren to open it for me, but she shook her head.

"I have a good feeling about this one, Mom. You open it," she told me.

As I pulled my passport from the envelope, I noticed, first of all, that there was no additional piece of paper as there had been before—just my passport. I thumbed through the first familiar pages, and then I saw it!

VISTO, Italia, from September 12, 2013, to September 11, 2014!

My knees gave out, and I started to cry. I had done it! I had the golden ticket to my new life in Italy right here in my hand! This had been my dream, my goal that I often thought was out of my reach, and in less than a month I would make it my reality. I thanked my angels for their obvious assistance. I was overjoyed!

I began to pack with the idea of being away from the U.S. for at least an entire year. I started buying aspirin and Clif Bars in bulk, as well as almond butter, gum, and cosmetics. I downsized even more and began donating clothing, shoes, and handbags—anything that wasn't absolutely essential. I tried to let the reality sink in that I would spend an entire, uninterrupted year in my beloved Italy.

Twenty-four

August in Laguna Beach is cooler than in Salt Lake City, and just an hour-and-a-half flight away. Sherrilee picked me up at the airport, and we headed to our favorite spot to have big salads on the patio. She was still hurting over the demise of her marriage, and I was worried about how much weight she'd lost and how sad she was.

We spent the first days together talking; we laughed and cried over how life had picked us up and thrown us down. Most of all, we found consolation in just being together. I asked her if she wanted to come to Italy and get away to heal with me there, but she said no. She had family close by and said Italy hadn't called to her as it had to me. I understood that.

One evening as Sherrilee and I sat on her patio drinking wine, my phone rang and I saw it was Lauren. I was surprised, as we had talked just an hour ago, and she had said she was headed to bed. As soon as I said hello, I could hear that she was crying. Through the emotion, she told me that a sheriff had come to her condo tonight with a summons for me.

I couldn't begin to imagine what any of it was about, thinking that most people didn't know where I was living, or even if I was back in Utah. I told her to open it and read me the contents.

Her voice was soft as she relayed to me that John, my ex-husband, was accusing me of violating the terms of alimony by cohabitation. In the summons was his demand for not only an immediate end to his requirement to pay alimony, but for me to repay him all that he'd paid since the date of the alleged cohabitation—several years' worth. He also asked me to pay his attorney fees along with several other fees that, in total, were more than my entire net worth.

I struggled to take the information in; I was not only confused, but it didn't seem real. I assured Lauren that there had been a misunderstanding somehow, and I would talk to an attorney tomorrow. She was embarrassed that all of her neighbors saw the sheriff at her door, and I was heartbroken that I wasn't there to help absorb that.

I said goodnight to Lauren and turned to see Sherrilee's waiting expression. She could tell from my side of the conversation that something was very wrong. I tried to explain to Sherrilee what I had just been told, but neither of us could grasp what was going on. I had been so particular in the decade after my divorce to always keep my house, utilities, everything in my name. I'd always paid all of my bills myself.

Thomas's work was in Salt Lake City a few days a week, and so he would often stay with me rather than make the commute to Saint George, about four hours away. I had been told by my lawyer at the time of my divorce that sleepovers between adults were fine, but each person needed to maintain their own primary residence and pay their own bills. I had always done that to the letter of the law.

The next morning I called Greg, the attorney who handled the divorce modification for me a couple of years ago. He asked me to have Lauren fax him the documents. He said he'd look them over right away and would call me back.

Sherrilee had run to the grocery store, so I was alone in the condo when Greg called me back.

"Who would want to throw you under the bus, Lisa?" he asked me.

I paused, as I couldn't think of anyone that would do something so hideous. Sure, I knew there were people who didn't like me, but I hadn't been the sort who created enemies along the way.

I was baffled as Greg explained that he'd talked to John's attorney, and while the other attorney wouldn't tell him who their witness was, he assured Greg that it was someone who knew enough that this would be an open-and-shut case.

"In other words," Greg pointed out, "this is someone who wants you to lose everything you have."

I sat in the silence with my mind racing but couldn't think of a single person.

He gently asked me again, "Lisa, who would do this to you?"

I had no idea. I know of no one who would wish to destroy me.

I was confused but told Greg that I'd make some calls, talk to Sherrilee, and see if I could come up with something. I knew he was counting on some direction from me, but I was clueless.

I sat alone on the bar stool in the kitchen and heard the wind chimes from the patio lightly clang through the open door. My chest felt hollow. I was unable to wrap my brain around doing such a vicious thing. As I sat and tried to formulate a concrete thought, I couldn't fathom who would reach out to John just to destroy me. And for what?

My concern then turned to Thomas. Oh, my God, he would surely be dragged into this, since it concerned where he slept, and I felt badly about that.

I found his number in my cell phone and called him.

Thomas didn't pick up my call, which seemed odd, given how he had tried to connect with me all summer. I decided to try again in a few minutes, as it wasn't the type of message I wanted to leave on his voice mail.

After calling Thomas several more times, I did leave a voice message saying that I would like to talk to him. When we finally did connect, I filled him in on what the accusations were and apologized for what may come, as I knew he would surely be questioned.

I was embarrassed, and told him so. He didn't say much, and I guessed he was still stinging from my email that had clearly spelled out that we were through. It was an awkward conversation, and he seemed to want to wrap it up quickly, and I did as well.

The next call I made was to Lauren and assured her it would all be fine. She was placed in a position that no child should ever face. A child's birthright should be parents who love them, no matter what happens in their marriage, and never place them in the middle. I had never placed either one of my children in a position to have to choose one parent over the other, or even talked poorly of their dad. I was saddened that he had sunk to a new low.

On an early-morning flight from Long Beach, I replayed the conversation I had with my attorney the previous night. Greg had told me that the opposing council was taking great pleasure in the strength of their case, and he asked me again who would throw me under the bus.

And then he asked, not for the first time, if I thought it could be Thomas.

I was certain it was not. For all of our arguments, and the eventual ugly ending, Thomas had never even met John. He had nothing to gain by delivering this type of financial blow to me. We weren't a couple any longer, and I couldn't imagine to what end this would serve him. Revenge?

At one time, I had wanted to marry Thomas. My mind drifted back to the times when his granddaughter had stayed at my house, when I had bathed her and rocked her to sleep. Those moments seemed so much more intimate than sex to me, acts of love in reaching out to another's family and making them your own. Love may change, couples break up, but at one time the love was real. I knew I still honored that and wondered if Thomas didn't.

While I couldn't yet think of Thomas very fondly yet, I certainly didn't wish him anything but happiness in his future, and I had to believe he would say the same for me.

Twenty-five

As I drove downtown to meet with my attorney, I was struck by how quickly I had gone back to being an all-American girl! Diet cola in the drink holder, classic rock on the radio, and me navigating the freeway—it was a world away from the life I led in the ancient city of Florence, but it was, of course, comfortable to me!

The first minutes of our meeting were spent catching up—life in Italy and life in Salt Lake. Greg felt more like a friend than the high-profile attorney he was, and I was so grateful for his kindness as well as his legal assistance.

We discussed that maybe this was just a bluff, thinking I'd get scared and fold my hand to walk away, leaving John a couple of thousand dollars richer each month. I had brought copies of all my bills, showing that I had paid for my own living accommodations, and ruminated over the ambiguity of Utah law regarding cohabitation.

It seemed an affront to me, first, to not have been able to receive the cash I was due at the time of divorcing so that I could live on my own without a continued attachment to my ex-husband. Utah law was archaic in this way, placing a dollar amount on a woman, depending on whether she slept alone or with someone else. For twenty-three years I was a full-time mother and wife, and the compensation should have been given at the end of the divorce and not still argued over years down the road.

There was no date set for the deposition yet, and I had let Greg know the date I was to leave for Italy. We chatted and laughed, and I left knowing my case was in good hands. My biggest concern was what it always had been with John and the legal system—he could afford to drag this out endlessly, and I could not.

My friend and former babysitter for my children, Sarah, came for coffee one morning in August with Lauren and me. She was in town for a high school reunion, and besides catching up, we talked about the business that I was now certain I was to organize in Italy.

Over our steaming mugs, Sarah listened as I described the feeling I had in Cortona. "I'm supposed to bring women to Tuscany, to let them experience the beauty and passion I have felt there," I told her. But living in Italy made it difficult for me to set up a business in the U.S., and we decided that would be where she came in! Sarah had experience in setting up businesses and was confident we could get one going.

I'd learned enough about Italy to know that business there worked via relationships—just ask the Mafia. Business relationships were solidified over coffee or lunch—not over the Internet. It was crucial for me to actually be in Tuscany, choosing the hotels, restaurants, guides, and drivers for the tour. I already had an idea of what I'd like to include for an eight-day, seven-night tour, and when Sarah asked when I thought the first one could be, I answered, "Next spring!"

The dog days of August in Utah are unbearably hot and sticky until finally a thunderstorm builds up over the Rocky Mountain range and plops down big drops of rain to cool off the valley. I am a fifth-generation Utahn, and I wondered on those August days about the mental stability of the pioneers who chose this desert to settle and make a new life!

I kept my daily focus on outlining the tour of Tuscany for the new company. I had spent a lot of time thinking about who our customers would be, how to attract women to our business who would want this experience, and how each day of the tour would unfold.

I was adamant that the company was to be for women who wanted to come to Tuscany not just as tourists, but to view the experience with a local. I wanted to share what I had found in Italy—an intimate experience of locals, art, food, joy, and passion.

I knew the devil was in the details, and I went through each day, each hour of the tour in minute detail. It kept my mind occupied with the future, and that kept me from wondering about what John was planning to throw my way.

As I began to pack my two suitcases for a full year away, I knew better this time what to pack in the limited space. Almond butter was something I started to crave after about a month, and vitamins, aspirin, and Aleve in the large bottles were worth the space they took up. I had learned to keep my clothing basic and pack lightly, with a new pair of Steve Madden Trooper boots to get me through the fall and winter months.

I felt the rise of anxiety when I thought about leaving my children for a full year, but the thrill of being able to stay in Italy, legally, for that long had my heart skipping happily! This was the opportunity I had been waiting for, and I had done the work to make it happen.

I listened to Pimsleur Italian on my morning walks, and it had me mentally preparing for my life in San Niccolò. It definitely offered a more traditional Italian experience.

I closed my eyes while I sat back in the rust-and-cream-colored floral chair in Lauren's condo, visualizing the apartment that was waiting for my arrival in less than a month. I remembered the windows most of all and the view out into a courtyard filled with plants, grass, and long tables. My bedroom window would overlook part of the Bardini Garden—a gorgeous space in Florence that connected to the Boboli Garden of Palazzo Pitti. I was thrilled with anticipation of life for a full year in this new space while I would work on a new business and share my love for Italy with other women. The pieces of my life seemed to be coming together for a life in Italy, and I was ready to head on home to Florence.

Twenty-six

Lauren and I flew down to visit Sherrilee in Laguna Beach at the end of August for a long weekend. Sherrilee's mom, Liz, and our friend, Shirlene, gathered one night for dinner and a knitting lesson! The lesson was for Lauren, who appeared to be a natural—not me.

We were all curled up on the white sofas and oversized chairs, sharing laughter and wine. My heart would swell when I looked at my girl sitting in between my dearest friend and Liz. There was sweetness and honesty forged among years of sharing our life together that made us a family, and I loved seeing my daughter join that.

I excused myself and stepped outside to take my attorney's call. Utah time is an hour ahead of California, so I was surprised to see Greg working so late. He told me that the date had been set for the deposition, and the witness had been revealed. Greg asked me if I could talk, and if I was sitting down.

I assured him I was fine, as I was outside of Sherrilee's condo in the beautiful last rays of sunlight from the day.

"Lisa," he said gently, "it's Thomas."

At that point, I wasn't processing what Greg was telling me, still feeling the lingering love and laughter from the knitting class inside.

"What?" I asked him.

"It's Thomas, Lisa. He contacted John a couple of months ago, met with him several times, and gave him all the information and dates necessary to establish cohabitation. He's thrown you under the bus." Greg was speaking slowly, but clearly. "Lisa, are you there?"

I could hear Greg's voice, but I couldn't respond. I felt that someone had just kicked me, hard, in the stomach, and I couldn't breathe.

If I could breathe, I would respond, I thought, but at that moment, I couldn't do either.

"Lisa, just let me know you understand what I said," Greg was imploring me for any sort of response.

"I can't breathe," I said in a whisper. "Don't hang up, I just can't breathe."

And in that moment, and the minutes that followed, Greg stayed with me as I leaned against the large oak tree in Sherrilee's front yard. The ground swirled below me, and the night sky was now dark.

"I know you never entertained the thought that it was Thomas, but I have wondered all along," said the man who had heard many confessions of the most brutal sort in his long career.

I knew there were mean men out there; I just had no idea that I had given my heart to two of them, who had now plotted together to essentially take me out financially and emotionally.

After repeated assurances that I had people around me, and I would go inside and talk to them, Greg let me hang up. I made an appointment to see him as soon as I returned to Salt Lake City, but that didn't keep the weight of betrayal from enveloping my body and settling in my chest, which felt too heavy and empty to take deep breaths.

I was having an out-of-body experience and seemed to be watching myself from a distant vantage point. I could see my lethargic frame leaning against the large tree and implored my legs to move, but they remained planted right next to the tree.

> *The saddest thing about betrayal is it never comes from your enemies.*
>
> —Ash Sweeney

I sat in my favorite floral chair in Lauren's condo in Salt Lake City for hours, playing Candy Crush. I was not answering many calls these days, but when a call came in from Lauren, I picked up. She asked me a series of questions, revolving around if I had eaten, showered, and been out of the floral chair yet that day.

I answered, honestly, "No."

Lauren told me how many hours it would be until she was home, and I nodded. She was my lifeline those days, as I was not functioning. My brain, my heart, my day-to-day life had all shut down. I was in shock and shattered with the grief of betrayal. I was frightened of the future, and my hands shook all day long. I was not capable of thinking the way these two men had, so I sat in a fog, in denial, in despair. I did know that in a matter of days, I had to function enough to get on a plane and fly to Italy, but at this point I couldn't imagine how that would happen.

And so I sat in the floral chair, in my pajamas and unwashed hair, and played Candy Crush for all the daylight hours.

Twenty-seven

I sat looking out the window at the lavender-streaked western sky two days before I left for Florence. I looked down at the visa pasted into my passport, so grateful to know I could stay in Italy as a legal resident for at least a year. I was exhausted from the grief I carried, worried about my future with no income, but grateful to be going to the one place in the world where I wanted to be.

My children had talked to their father, reminding him that I was their mother and deserved to be treated with respect, as well as have a roof over my head. Their sadness and anger broke my heart all over again. I felt their love for me, and I knew they valued my role as their mom both in the past and the present. I wished I could spare them this harsh side of their dad, but I couldn't spare any of us. In his world of values, money was paramount and feelings were lower on the list.

I trusted Greg, and I knew I was in good hands. He had encouraged me to just get on the plane and go forward with my life. The few people who truly knew what was happening were appalled, but that did nothing to make me feel better. I found no pleasure in their heaping disdain on two men whom I left years ago. I chose to live life without them, and to them, that choice was unforgivable.

I was, for the most part, too distracted and tired for big goodbyes to friends, and they understood. The Dodo girls had all come by or called, and their constant love was a support for which there are no words. Jane planned to visit me at the end of October, and Lelan would come in the day before Jane left, and I was comforted knowing that.

My flight was the following evening, but on this day, I was up early and actually made it through the shower and got dressed! There was a drive I wanted to make before I left, a place I wanted to see, and I wanted to see it badly enough that I was making myself function.

Although I hadn't been there for years, I knew the road to take once I was inside the Brigham City Cemetery. Nestled in the far east side of the vast expanse of grass was where my extended family had their final resting places. The trees were old now and large enough to cast some shade on the section I was seeking—Jensen.

I parked the car and stepped out into the family plot, wishing I'd brought some flowers for my grandmother. But the only flowers that reminded me of her were lilacs, and their season had passed. I walked among the headstones of those I knew and others I knew only by name.

My two cousins, closest to me in age, were here, having left this earth far too early. My Aunt Ruthe was here, who lost her husband, mother, and son in the space of five years. My sweet Aunt Miriam was there adjacent to her son, Mark, who was closest to me in age.

I finally felt I could exhale as I walked among the headstones. This was my tribe, those who came before me, faced their own hardships and joys, and then left us. I smiled as I recalled Thanksgiving dinners and summers at the swimming pool with my cousins, aunt, and uncle in Brigham City.

Once I found who I was looking for, the tears welled up in my eyes, and I knelt down by their headstones. While I never knew my great-grandmother, Martha, I was told stories of her by my grandmother, until she came to life for me not only as a heroine, but a beloved part of my history.

My great-grandmother had been raised in polygamy with twelve other brothers and sisters. After marrying and having four children, she was widowed at the young age of twenty-nine. While the custom of the time was to place widows into other Mormon families by plural marriage, she would have none of it. She sewed, took in ironing, and cooked for others, and she made a living for her children while she lived independently of another marriage.

My grandmother, my Mema, would often pat my hand as she recalled the hardships faced by her young mother and remind me, as always, "You come from a long line of strong women, Lisa."

Now as I rested my hand on my Mema's headstone, I was overcome with weariness. I told her how tired I was of betrayal and hurt, and how afraid I was of the future. I explained to her, as though she were seated right there with me, that I was leaving for life in a foreign country, and I didn't know when I would ever be back to visit her here.

I cried as I expressed to her how alone I felt, how overwhelming life was at that moment to me. I longed for the days when the two of us had sat together outside on her porch swing, holding hands while a rice pudding bubbled up in the oven, and she had expressed her complete adoration and love for me.

I could feel her sweet presence all around me and could actually smell the scent of lilacs floating through on a small breeze. I wondered if I could perhaps just join them, and celebrate being all together once more! But as quickly as that thought emerged, I heard her tell me to stand up on my own two feet and move forward.

"Our women are not the quitting, timid sort," she seemed to remind me. "They have always met life head-on with an open heart but a formidable presence."

On that day, all alone in the cemetery, I felt their DNA course through my veins, and while I may not have known what was ahead, I knew where I came from. I was from a long line of strong women, and so I told these beloved family members goodbye and got back in my car to drive home.

Twenty-Eight

Justin arrived in the afternoon to take me to the airport. My two suitcases held all I would have for the next year, and pretty much all I had in the world! I left some files and documents with Lauren, but other than that I had pared down to carrying just what would fit in two bags. It felt good to travel so lightly and unencumbered.

Saying goodbye to my girl was always hard, but this time I could see in her eyes that she was worried about me. "I'll be fine, baby," I told her, needing to convince both of us.

As much as I hated to leave her and knew that she wasn't speaking to her dad, I also knew that I wasn't any good to her at that time.

I am broken, I thought as I closed the top of the suitcase. *I need to heal myself before I can help anyone else.* My mind felt bruised and foggy and my body heavy and tired. I couldn't remember the last time I had eaten—or smiled.

Just follow Justin to the car, I thought as I walked behind my son, squinting in the sunshine, as he carried my suitcases to the car. *Just get in the car, get through security, and on the plane. Next time you have to function, you'll be in Europe.* That thought alone kept me going.

I checked my suitcases in with the skycap and hugged Justin goodbye, holding him for what seemed like a full minute. His plan was that his work would send him to Europe in November, and he would spend Thanksgiving with me.

Right now that seemed forever away, but I was happy to have relieved him of the pain of seeing me so sad. Both of my children looked unhappy and so worried about me, and I wanted to put an ocean of distance between myself and that.

I glanced up at the Wasatch Mountains and quickly turned away, walking into the Salt Lake City airport to take my flight to Paris and then to Florence, Italy.

I don't care if I never see this airport or this city again, I thought as I made my way through the sliding doors of the Salt Lake International Airport.

Walking down the aisle of the plane, I saw my seatmate was already settled. I lifted my carry-on bag into the overhead bin and excused myself as I slid into the window seat. I could never decide which was the lesser of two evils: having to climb over legs and a sleeping body to use the restroom, or not having a place to rest my head on the long flight.

I reached in my purse for my iPod and headphones, to make it clear I'm not the chatty type of passenger, and tucked my purse down in front of me. I was already thinking about the two glasses of wine I would rapidly consume with a little dinner and the long nap I planned to take over the ocean. I decided to not be a total bear and offered my seatmate a weak smile and hello as I settled in and unwrapped my blanket.

"Are you leaving home, or going home?" she asked me in a perky voice and sweet smile.

"Hmmm," I said, meeting her gaze.

I'm pretty sure she didn't think she'd asked a trick question, and yet, there I was struggling for an answer. Was I going home, or leaving my home? I looked out the small window of the airplane and studied the outline of the Wasatch Mountains while I steadied my voice.

The westernmost range of the greater Rocky Mountains spanning almost one- hundred-and-sixty miles, those mountains served as the background scenery to most of the events of my life. Even when I had moved away from Salt Lake City at times, I had always known I would return. I could count on the airplane dropping down, about ten minutes prior to landing, to give me a bird's-eye view of the jagged granite walls that made up my beloved mountains. And at that moment, I would know I was home. I could feel it deep in my bones as if those granite walls were part of my DNA. This flight was the first time in my life that there was no return trip planned.

My mind shifted from the granite walls of Salt Lake City to the terracotta rooftops of Florence, Italy. For the first time in weeks, I felt excitement. Now I ached to see a sunset over the Arno River, to hear the sound of opera blasting from an apartment window. Would it ease my pain and let my heart feel joy again? Could the rhythm of Italian life, where the bells served as my alarm clock, bring me back to life?

"I think I'm going home," I finally answered. I let out a long exhale, and the elephant on my chest shifted slightly. *Going home to carve out a new life in a very old country,* I thought to myself.

Upon arriving in Florence, I didn't have a working cell phone to contact the agent of my apartment. I had given her an approximate time I would be there, but now I was dependent on the kindness of my taxi driver to let me use his cell phone and place a call.

My Italian was rusty, and I'd already asked him to lift two very heavy suitcases, but his natural Italian kindness took over, and he easily agreed to let me call. When I called the agency, Adriana assured me that she would be at my apartment to welcome me and give me the keys, and so, tired as I was, I felt like the long journey was mostly behind me.

I arrived at the building on the Oltrarno side of town, which was to be my new home, and Adriana buzzed me through the giant door and then the interior gates. I had to drag each suitcase up fifty-six steps to my apartment, and I knew it would take every last drop of energy I had. As I finally dragged the last one, lift and drop, to the front of the wooden door, I rang the bell while perspiration trickled down my back.

Adriana greeted me with kisses and led me inside the apartment for a quick tour and signing of papers. On my best day, I couldn't have understood how to use the TV remote—just ask my kids—but on this day, her directions were useless.

I followed her around like a dutiful puppy, even nodding at the appropriate times, but nothing sank in. Once we said goodbye and the door closed, I collapsed in a deflated purple chair by the dining room table.

Suitcases would remain packed tonight, and if I was to stay awake to even seven o'clock, I knew I needed to get outside and walk. I hadn't the stamina to face a grocery store, so I strolled down my block to a lively area of restaurants and bars. There was a corner just outside the steep path to the Rose Garden and Piazzale Michelangelo that was always filled with young people, energy, and amazing aromas from the surrounding *osterias* and bars.

As I rounded the corner from San Niccolò, the smell of pizza drew me into a restaurant called BevoVino. In my jet-lagged stupor, I walked in and sat at the bar to order a pizza to go.

"You look like you could use a cold glass of *prosecco*," the young man who was waiting on me, and everyone else, said.

"Okay," was all I could reply.

As I peeked into the kitchen, I could tell something had been lost in translation. The pizza I had asked for, with two ingredients, had become *two* pizzas. Perhaps it was the *prosecco* or just that eating two pizzas for the next few days sounded fine to me, but I sat on the barstool and smiled as Vincenzo, my server, refilled my glass with another *prosecco.*

I walked back to my new apartment and could feel the last of the day's sunshine hit my back, feel the warmth of my two pizzas in their boxes on my hands, and felt my spirits lifted by my vibrant new neighborhood. Once inside my apartment, and a couple of pieces of pizza later, I couldn't hold out any longer. I washed my face and climbed in the cool, crisply ironed sheets of my bed.

I could hear the sounds of neighbors having dinner, lively music coming in from below my window, and, from a distance, a TV blaring in Italian.

All of it could go on without me; I had to go to sleep.

At two thirty-seven a.m., I woke up—such was the joy of traveling halfway around the world. I walked to the bedroom window and opened the green shutters to see the outline of palm trees in the shimmering moonlight. Clouds moved in and out of the moon's light and a slight rustle of leaves was all that interrupted the absolute silence of the night.

I took a deep breath in and allowed the moonlight and stillness to wash over me.

"Welcome home," I whispered, breaking the quiet of the summer's night. I'd made it home!

I was home and I was hungry—and there was a pizza and a half waiting for me in the fridge.

Twenty-nine

September 2013

While my attorney and I were in contact, the time difference made it difficult to connect and talk very often. Greg would depose Thomas in a couple of days, and with that, we would know what I was up against. The betrayal seemed to hit me freshly in the stomach each time I thought of it, and I wondered how it was that I had once loved two men who would like to see me kicked to the curb without a dime.

The weather was warmer in Florence than in Salt Lake, and I found it quickly sapped whatever bit of energy I started out with in the morning. I'd left to purchase a few groceries from Sant'Ambrogio Market, plus wine and coffee, and then dragged myself home. I decided I'd rather drink tap water than haul bottles of water up fifty-six steps, then engaged in a Google search to see if a restaurant or café anywhere in Florence delivered food.

I sat in my purple chair with the flat cushions and looked out at the Bardini Garden and the small patch of grass below, where my young neighbor, perhaps two or three years old, frequently came out to play. He chased his cat until the cat grew weary of it and scaled the rock wall or his mother would come out to sweep him up in her arms and carry him back inside.

My mind drifted back to the days of young children, with the endless laundry and meals…and laughter and love. How

I had loved to be with my young ones! I'd relished the summer days of playing outside, baths at night, and fresh pajamas for bedtime. I loved the smell of their heads as I held them close to me, the stories we read together, and the security I had known when we were all under one roof.

I realized, as I saw the golden light reflecting on the palm trees, that it must be evening. I'd sat in my robe, in this chair, the entire day. The depth of my sadness scared me on those days, as depression was not something I had a lot of experience with, and it appeared endless. I felt utterly without hope, and I wondered, as I continued to stare out my window, if that was the definition of depression—to be utterly without hope.

I knew I needed to organize my mind around creating my new business and think about tours of Tuscany for women, as well as prepare for Jane's and Lelan's visits, but I found my body too lethargic and sad to move. I waited to hear from Greg as to what transpired in my absence in Salt Lake City.

Thomas gave testimony that sought to negate John's obligation to send me any money and, in fact, I was asked to pay John back several years' worth of alimony.

Greg sent me emails, and as we communicated, I was suspended in disbelief yet again. Thomas and John had met several times over drinks, Thomas had gleefully reported on the stand. He'd gladly shared with John that he had stayed at my house while he rented his, and he had the rental receipts to prove it. These two men, Greg told me, would stop at nothing to destroy me.

I let that sink in. These two men would stop at nothing to destroy me.

Greg walked me through my choices, and I tried to listen and follow his words. Option one—I could return to Salt Lake City and fight this through the legal system. He gave me a fifty-fifty chance of winning, depending on the judge who heard the case. While I can definitely show that I paid my own bills and kept my own place of residence, Thomas showed proof that he shared that space for six weeks. He apparently didn't mention that he had also kept all the money he received in rent revenue from his Saint George condo. John, of course, had lived with his partner for years, bought a home with her, and moved forward in his life. That, however, didn't matter in the courts of Utah.

But whatever their need or reasons were for revenge, ego or bravado, I closed the door to my heart on it all. I couldn't process fighting or going back to Salt Lake. Thomas and John were, apparently, great friends—a united front of hate, with one common goal and enemy: me.

Greg told me that if I didn't choose to fight the case, alimony would stop immediately. He fought to keep John from going after more money in the way of legal fees and past payments made. I could tell he thought this was the best option as he gently broke it to me that I no longer had any income.

And then Greg spoke to me as a friend—not an attorney. "Go after this chance to be happy, Lisa," he said kindly, "and don't look backward."

I told him I couldn't leave Italy, as I had nothing left in me to fight these two. They won, and I would stay in Italy—my place of peace and happiness.

I thanked Greg, and even as he was saying that he'd send all the documents and files of resolution, I knew I would never read them. I didn't have the heart, or stomach, to know any more of the details than I already did. I had no desire, then or now, to read a transcript of a man giving testimony for no other reason than revenge. Somewhere in my soul, survival had to kick in.

I would have wailed at the moon about justice if I'd had the strength, but I did not. I was blindsided by the two men I had loved most in the world as they joined forces to humiliate and bankrupt me. I knew I could either stay in the corner, beat up and defeated, or choose to live. My hope that night was that I had the strength to choose the latter.

I knew what Greg charged per hour, and while I was afraid to ask what I owed him, it was only fair that he was paid for the work he'd done. I asked him to send me a bill and told him I would pay him from my account in the U.S.

"It has been my pleasure to represent you, Lisa," he said kindly. "You won't be receiving a bill from me. I think you are truly a good person, and I hope you will stop by to say hello if you are ever back in Utah."

With those words of kindness and grace, I found the sliver of strength to take a deep breath and start again.

Year Two ~ 2013

Prologue

Like any love affair, the shine eventually wears off and reality sets in. Painful, to be sure, but a necessary part of the transition of any long-lasting romance.

Italy's particular slap of reality was confusing, because it came with so many contradictions. Just as I was certain I understood how *they* thought or how *that* worked, the opposite would simultaneously occur, leaving me more bewildered than when I started.

Sure, I'd had men play me for a fool before—but never a nation!

In a country that revolves around and reveres the family, extramarital affairs are casually accepted. Infidelity doesn't raise an eyebrow but rather receives the common shoulder shrug along with the "what are you going to do" expressionless expression.

Catholic culture permeates all aspects of Italian culture, but few seem to actually follow the tenets of their faith. Marriages and birth rates are on a steady decline, and few seem to take the cautionary words from the Vatican too seriously.

The world flocks to Italy to experience the *dolce vita*, but Italians consistently rank themselves as the least happy nation in Europe. Ask an Italian how they are doing and the answer will generally be that things could be better—a lot better. And then they will spend the next twenty minutes telling you how with both words and gestures.

Italy became a unified country in 1861, not that long ago in its history, and divisions are evident along social and economic lines. The idea of one Italy, from the striking Alps to the warm beaches of Sicily, simply doesn't exist within the Italian mind.

In a country smaller in square miles than California, Italy is a mix-master of languages. While outsiders marvel at the beauty of Italian, the *bella lingua*, a common language doesn't exist. Dialects are spoken in many different regions, and some are considered separate languages altogether. Italians speak with their hands just to communicate with other Italians of different regions!

I was now in my second year in Italy, and I had started to understand the magic and mirrors involved in the frequently discussed *bella figura*. I had reveled in Italians' love of beautiful clothes and manners my first year here, but year two revealed that there was something more underhanded.

The *bella figura*, the quest to present a beautiful presence, is as much an individual quest as a nation's desire. It's basically: Do it all perfectly, and don't let them see you sweat! Present a package so beautifully wrapped that the tourists will happily tiptoe around filthy sidewalks. Dress up in Gucci, Prada, and Fendi, and we can all ignore the rampant unemployment rate!

As I labored my way through the labyrinth of bureaucracy during year two, in acquiring my first *Permesso di soggiorno,* my head swam in disbelief. There was no one answer, one solution, or any set of guidelines that could streamline the process.

A trip to the post office to ask a question about the forms (yes, one goes to the post office to get *permesso* forms) could take all afternoon. It will involve coffee breaks (theirs, not yours), line intruders, and at least one full-on meltdown (again, theirs—not yours).

My version of the *dolce vita* had soured in a hurry. I was beginning to see why so many of the expats I had enthusiastically met my first year here had returned to their English-speaking homelands.

Living here on a full-time basis took grit, tenacity, and a certain amount of stubbornness. And while enduring all the difficulties, remember the paramount rule: Never let them see you sweat. It could be exhausting.

But the second year in Italy brought me Italian friends, a new business, and an underlying certainty that this was home. For better or for worse, I had taken my vows with Italy quite seriously.

Thirty

I was up before the first ray of light, as it was the day I was to visit the Questura for my *Permesso di soggiorno*. I had filled out the Italian paperwork that accompanied my visa and paperwork from the U.S., and this morning was my assigned day to submit my *permesso* at the police headquarters.

Although my appointment time was 10:19 (not 10:15 or 10:20), I had been told by other expats to arrive early and get a number.

I wasn't exactly certain where the Questura was, and knowing it would be difficult to locate in the dark of early morning, I gave myself a rare treat of taking a taxi. As the taxi stopped in front of the office, I opened my door to see a long line had already formed outside the red brick building.

I waited with them, the mass of humanity standing in line to achieve permission. Our common goal this morning was permission to legally live in Italy. We were united in our morning haziness, under the first pink streaks of daylight.

Together we waited outside the building to secure our places in line. A line that would move forward and give us a number that would then direct us to a window where someone would determine whether or not we had sufficiently met all the requirements for permission. We had secured visas from our home countries, but now we asked our new country for its permission.

To me, as I waited outside in the chilly morning air, the entire process felt more like *stand up; sit down; jump here; turn around; now sit down again*. But what did I know?

The line began to move—thankfully, as it was warmer inside the corridor. We were each given a number and then directed to two different lines. The men that worked there spoke only Italian, and I tried to process what I was told.

"Here's your number" and "after eight o'clock" is about all I comprehended from the officer's Italian. Unsure as to where to go, I turned back to ask. However, it was too late, as someone else had already moved up, and apparently there was no time for questions.

I spotted another long line and dutifully took my place in it. An officer came by, tapped me on the shoulder, and said something to me in rapid Italian.

Seriously, I thought to myself, *does he think I've had enough coffee or Italian to understand that?*

The wheels slowly started to turn in my sluggish brain, however. He'd said something about this not being my line. I was in the wrong line! I was supposed to go inside, find a seat, and watch for my number to appear over one of the cubicles.

As I sat down on the steel bench, I thought about how hard I had worked to be here. Each person I saw had done the same. I knew that each one of us arrived on our appointed day, ticket in hand, with a personal story of desire.

That desire was to make our life in a country in which we were not born.

A woman approached the seat next to me and began to vigorously wipe it down with sanitizer. I guessed she knew something I did not. I just plopped myself right down.

A beautiful woman from the Middle East, her head wrapped in a scarf, sat down on the bench across from me with her young daughters. I wondered how early they had awakened that day to be here before seven a.m. The baby called out from her stroller, and immediately the mother looked up.

Mothers. The world over, we instinctively respond to our baby's voice.

My thoughts drifted to my own ancestors who immigrated to the United States from Denmark. They had embraced a new religion and wanted to join with other members in the American West.

I thought again of my great-great grandmother who made the arduous trip across the ocean, and then across the plains of the United States. Coffee and her morning paper were a constant, no matter where she lived nor which religion she joined.

"One can only make so many sacrifices," she would say in her defense.

I was thinking I could use another cup of coffee about then.

"You are from a long line of strong women, Lisa," rang in my ears now. I hadn't given it much thought until the past decade. Now I depended on it.

Nearing eight a.m., the waiting area filled up. It was utilitarian and cold. I listened to the conversation of two men from Africa behind me. The sounds and clicking noises were exotic and so foreign to my ears.

The mother across from me discreetly fed her baby. A tiny hand reached up out of a pink sweater to hold her mother's. Such a moment of beauty.

As I waited under the harsh white lights, my mind drifted to my babies, now thirty-two and twenty-nine years old. I wondered if they were sound asleep half a world away. I wished I could peek at their faces. What lessons would they learn from me and pass down to their children? Would the family's stories recall crazy Grandma Lisa who took off for Italy and never came back?

I looked in the eyes of people of every color. Everyone had a story that brought us to a point this morning where our lives intersected for a minute. Everyone looked a little hesitant, a little worried. There was a lot on the line.

I had heard the other expats' experiences of their day here. I had to apply twice to get my U.S. visa, so I was a little nervous. Did I think of absolutely every document they may ask to see?

My number was announced, and I approached the appropriate window. My heart was beating rapidly, and I tried to not have too much emotion show on my face.

After brief greetings and the exchange of my passport, the woman started to have me sign papers. I didn't question. I signed. She got up and disappeared behind a partition. Returning, she handed me a sheet of paper and explained that I needed to attend a culture class on December 6.

"Failure to do so results in diminished points," she told me.

"Um, okay," I answered, not having a clue as to what she was talking about.

"You will be notified when your card is ready for pickup," she said. It was all in Italian. Was I missing something?

"*Si,*" I replied.

We stared at each other. I was trying to determine what was happening.

"*Ho finito?*" (Have I finished?) I asked.

"*Si,*" she answered without expression.

"*Veremente?*" (Really?) I asked, my face now overflowing with emotion.

"*Si,*" and she smiled a little.

Hey, who am I to argue? I thought to myself.

I gathered the thick file of documents I brought with me, none of which I had to produce, and headed toward the door.

"I did it!" I said softly to myself as I walked out.

I had been granted a *Permesso di soggiorno*! Permission to live in Italy for a full year! Just as my ancestors before me, I set out on a journey to live in a new land, and I had just crossed the equivalent of Ellis Island! Once outside, I couldn't contain myself any longer. Finally, some good news, and I started to laugh as I walked back home!

Thirty-one

There will come a time when you believe everything is finished. That will be the beginning.

—Mark Nepo

The October air was slightly cooler, and my heart seemed less heavy. I decided to take one of my favorite walks, to the church of San Miniato on a hill overlooking Florence.

The road leading up to the Rose Garden, Piazzale Michelangelo, and San Miniato was right in my neighborhood and had been quietly calling to me for days. As I made my way down the narrow street of San Niccolò, I followed the curve in the road and stopped to take in the view. I looked back toward my building in at what seemed like a painting—ancient buildings, iron lampposts, neon graffiti, and a burst of flowers.

Around the corner was BevoVino, where I had ordered pizza in my jet-lagged stupor my first evening back in Florence. I was a regular in those months, dropping in once or twice a week, and Enzo would look up with a smile and a glass of prosecco, just as he had that night. Always polite and kind, whether we spoke in Italian or English, Vincenzo ensured I was not overlooked in the ocean of locals that filled the small space nor lost in the throng of tourists drifting in.

I found that most places on the Oltrarno side of the river did not cater to tourists in the way Central Florence does, and it pushed me to speak more Italian and be more assertive.

The Panino & Vino shop was no bigger than a closet, with amazing options for panini with spreads, meats, cheeses, and vegetables. One of their sandwiches was easily two meals for me and, at four euro, a bargain! The owners were curious, at first, about a woman from the U.S. who had chosen to make her life here, in the Oltrarno area of Florence. Soon, however, I came to know Dominic and Francesca, who were warm and friendly as I spoke my broken Italian with them. Neither one spoke any English, but our exchanges were always happy breaks in my day. They knew I lived just up the street, and although they wondered about my solo status, (which they regularly checked up on), they would greet me enthusiastically and made me feel like part of the neighborhood.

My energy had been lacking some on this morning as I stretched my stride out to match the long steps up to the piazzale, but it felt so good to my soul. Movement is my comfort zone; it's how I have spent so much of my life—dancing, running, and teaching fitness classes. I knew the benefits were mental as well, so I pushed myself to continue up the final flight of stairs beyond the Rose Garden.

Most tourists stop at Piazzale Michelangelo for the view of Florence, which is fabulous, but an even better view is available about seven minutes beyond. While the steps seemed to be unending, the view from San Miniato al Monte was magnificent! I practiced counting in Italian as I took on each new stair, trying to distract my mind from the climb. My legs tingled as I made the final approach, my chest heaving, but I knew I could make it!

As I reached the church on the mountaintop, I walked to a small stone wall and looked over the valley below. From Santa Croce to the Duomo, the Medici Chapels to the hills of Fiesole, and all five bridges, Florence stood in its glory! I lived in one of the most beautiful cities on earth! I took a deep breath and let that thought wash over me. I lived in Florence, Italy, and it felt like home to me!

On this morning I had let go of the perpetual worry of how I was going to make it, financially, and simply basked in the warmth of the fall weather. The sky was a brilliant blue, and the scent of the rich earth filled my nostrils as I kicked through the fallen leaves on the path outside the church.

I turned to walk into San Miniato, knowing the wide plaster walls, few windows, and high ceilings would make the temperature drop from the outside heat. Inside, I was almost alone and my footsteps echoed as I walked toward a bench to sit down. I tried to quiet my heavy breathing for fear it would echo inside the massive church as well.

As I sat among the frescoes and lingering scent of incense, I gazed up at the beams forming the ceiling and over to the huge mural, which, even without lights, glittered with its gold mosaic.

I closed my eyes and began to pray, silently. (I would get down on the prayer bench if they were padded, I told my angels, but my knees couldn't take it!) I had a feeling prayers are heard wherever they are offered.

Finally, on that October morning, my prayers were not uttered in sadness nor longing for the pain to stop. On this day, my prayers were filled with gratitude. There was the physical reminder, with the perspiration on my brow and my still-shaking legs, that I was still very much alive.

For whatever the past month has thrown at me, I thought, *I am alive. I am in Florence. I am. Thank you.*

I told my angels, as my breath began to slow down, that I didn't think they would lead me this far to fail. I trusted that I was answering a call, a passion, a curiosity that had led me here.

I was working hard to create a business where I could share the beauty of Tuscany with other women, and I knew I would write.

"I think I have a message to share," I whispered to the ancient walls, "and I will find a way back again to my own joy."

I walked from the main area of the church, down a few steps, and into the oldest part of the crypt in San Miniato. Candles flickered in the cave-like basement, and I was enveloped with a feeling of peace. I may not have known what the future would hold, or how I was to carve it out, but I knew

I wasn't alone. And, as I passed through the massive wooden doors of the church, I looked down to see a perfect white feather on the step.

Thirty-two

On a morning in late October, I traveled to Santa Croce with my dear friend Jane. Her arrival had brought fresh energy to my apartment as well as to my business plans. She bravely evicted a couple of geckoes that I couldn't (or didn't dare) catch, along with several spiders. I appreciated that living next to the Bardini Garden was beautiful, but a few more critters sneaked through the open windows than I was used to.

Jane and I went to high school together and then lived in the same sorority house at Utah State, so our friendship was easy and the comfort developed over decades. Jane's red hair and charismatic personality drew people of any country to her. She listened intently and laughed easily, and I observed how quickly she put total strangers at ease.

Jane was coming with me to explore different walking tours, day adventures outside of Florence, and, of course, restaurants. We had a full schedule ahead of us this week, and it began today on a tour with Alexandra Lawrence.

My landlady, Adriana, had written to me about a British woman who had recently arrived in Florence and was in need of some English-speaking friends. This was a common occurrence, and I was equally delighted and amazed at how open and inclusive the expat group was. After spending almost my entire life in Salt Lake City, I hadn't realized until my move here how necessary it is to connect and quickly be assimilated when you are the new person in town. I invited Pat, the newcomer, via email to join Jane and me on our tour with Alexandra and to lunch afterward.

Jane was as impressed with Alexandra as I had been, and I was certain after this morning that I wanted her to lead the introductory walking tour of Florence for the ladies of my tour group. Alexandra had an ability to make history come to life, and I found I was totally captivated by her stories and vast knowledge of the Medici, Dante, and a thousand other subjects I had never studied in or out of school!

Pat wasn't difficult to identify once she said a few words! Her English accent was a total giveaway, and I immediately liked her. Petite, blonde, with twinkling eyes, she was overjoyed to be in Florence and had retired from her job just a week before her arrival here! At lunch, we shared the "short versions" of how we had come to be in a foreign country. We made plans to meet during the week to explore San Marco and try a new restaurant for lunch. Pat felt like an old friend immediately. There was something familiar about her to me, as though we'd shared a previous lifetime together and had agreed in this one to meet again.

"Ooooh Lisa, that would be just *fab!*" she exclaimed, and I laughed at hearing an expression straight out of the sixties.

In the weeks before Jane arrived, I began writing—a lot. When I shared mass emails about my new life in Florence with friends the previous year, I heard back from many of them. Writing had helped me process darker days, but I started to think about ways to share my thoughts on my new life in Italy with a wider audience. It would be a great form of advertising for the business as well as a possible avenue for future income.

The obvious choice for the first piece of writing was how a middle-aged American woman of Danish descent sold most of her earthly possessions to take a giant leap of faith. I worked on the writing, edited and read it over several times, and considered it just about ready to share. I had never been a writer and felt very timid about throwing my personal work into the arena of professionals. The story seemed personal, and I hesitated sending it out in cyberspace for anyone to see.

Lelan would arrive right after Jane's ten-day visit, so I knew this new creative outlet would take a backseat to travel for a while. But I was intrigued by how much I enjoyed the creative process of putting thoughts into words and the satisfaction when the story felt complete.

For the next three weeks, two of my dearest friends in turn accompanied me all over Tuscany and beyond! We explored famous and not-so-famous cities, from Cinque Terre to Assisi, Rome to Venice, and, of course, Florence. These two "advisors" were instrumental in helping me map out our signature tours of Tuscany as we chose the very best of the best. I was slowly feeling joy seep back into my soul as I shared my new home with old friends.

Back in the U.S., Sarah was setting up a website, working on payment plans, and opening business accounts. My mind buzzed with the plethora of activities and trips that could make up a tour of this region, and I acknowledged to myself on a daily basis what a pleasant change this month was from the last.

In drawing up an itinerary for the tour, not only did I need to determine the cost but also come to grips with the fact that most guests couldn't take three months off to visit! I had difficulty paring the tour down to just eight days and seven nights, knowing that ladies would be making the trip of a lifetime and may never return. But the biggest question that haunted me was the practical one: Would anyone really sign up to come on a tour?

Jane and I took the train to Cortona and stayed the night. We explored Le Celle, the retreat of Saint Francis, Bramasole, and all over the quaint hill town. Mariano picked us up at the train station and insisted on taking us to dinner in Camucia for pizza. He promised it would be the best we'd ever had, and both Jane and I agreed—it was.

The following morning, on a picture-perfect day in Tuscany, we planned to visit a couple of different wineries. The colors of fall were muted against the bright blue sky, as the grapes were finally ready for harvest. It was remarkable to see the process, smell the fermenting grapes, and get a sense of each winery's personality.

We joined with another group in the gorgeous tasting area of the Villa Sant'Anna winery. Owned and run by women, our hostess was the regal Simona Ruggeri-Fabroni and her daughters, Anna and Margherita. They exemplified the timeless, classic dress and manners of Italian women. Gracious in opening up their family business to visitors, they responded as most Italians do, to formal conversation and not casual friendliness.

While we were being generously served wine, cheeses, and bread, the couples around me raved about the villa where they stayed and its owner, Vittorio Cambria. They described it as something out of a movie—huge, impressive, with every luxury. And they were buying a lot of wine from Sant'Anna, which had Simona calling to her daughter to bring out a bottle of Vin Santo!

I leaned over to tell Jane that Vin Santo was a dessert wine used to dip biscotti, or *cantuccini*. I was quickly corrected by one of Simone's daughters, who explained that while most Vin Santo is used for dipping, theirs is NOT! Graciously I accepted my scolding, and then tasted the golden liqueur. Typically I am not a big fan of any dessert wine, but I had never tasted anything like this! Not overly sweet, but oh so smooth, I understood why the cost was what it was at Sant'Anna for a bottle of Vin Santo! I also knew why there was no need to add a cookie to the experience of drinking this liquid gold.

We prepared to leave when I was approached by a large, burly Italian man who asked me if I was Lisa, the lady who runs tours. Someone in his group had told him I was an American lady living in Florence, and he introduced himself as Vittorio, the owner of a villa outside Siena. We quickly exchanged business cards, and he promised I'd hear from him during the next week.

As Lelan arrived, Jane was packing to leave. We'd had a whirlwind couple of weeks traveling and touring, and we brought Lelan up to speed over a dinner of pasta and wine. She would be the next one to travel with me, and the feedback and encouragement from both of them gave me great confidence in my new business venture, as well as much-needed companionship.

Lelan was another sister/friend,who I'd known since college. With her glowing olive skin, and blonde hair, it took her all of five minutes to get a marriage proposal from an Italian man selling purses in the San Lorenzo market. She was a gentle person who rarely passed judgment on anyone, so her complete condemnation of Thomas and my ex-husband kept me laughing!

Vittorio's email, along with his invitation to come to Villa Ferraia, arrived a couple of days later. He wanted to know if I would take the train to Siena where he would pick me up. I wrote back that I had a friend staying with me, but if I could bring her along, we'd be happy to come.

We had set the date for just a couple of days away, and I told Lelan that I had no idea what the adventure would bring, but spending a couple of hours in Siena shopping wouldn't be bad, no matter what happened with Vittorio. Lelan laughed at my total trust in a total stranger, but for me, it was normal to set off, albeit blindly, into the unknown.

I always liked the train ride to Siena, with the beautiful Tuscan countryside for scenery and eavesdropping on Italian conversations. Vittorio arrived to pick us up in a large SUV and was gregarious and charming. Conversation was easy, his English impeccable. At the train station we were about thirty minutes away from the villa.

I jumped in the front and Lelan in the back behind Vittorio. He relayed the history of Villa Ferraia, how he came to own this centuries-old estate, and how he had developed an international clientele. I was immediately impressed by Vittorio's brilliant mind and his vision for attracting business.

We exited the freeway a good way from Siena and continued to take one smaller road after another. Eventually we were going through a wooded area so dense it was impossible to see through. The road was winding, and I glanced over at Vittorio and then back to make eye contact with Lelan.

I realized, with a sudden pit in my stomach, that I didn't know anything about who this man was, or where we were going. Furthermore, yet again, I had taken off on another adventure without telling anyone in Florence the details. I glanced at Vittorio's massive hands, which he had gripped around the steering wheel, and wondered what I had gotten not only myself, but my dear friend, into.

We left the paved road and continued along on a bumpy dirt one, which Vittorio navigated with expertise. As the large vehicle crossed a narrow stream on an even narrower bridge, he let us know we were close. I let out a little sigh of relief and checked in with Lelan with my eyes. I could see she had become equally apprehensive, and very quiet.

Once we approached the gate, our host entered a pass code, and the massive gate swung open. We veered left, and then up a slight hill, and I began to see the top of the villa. Vittorio honked to signal our approach as I looked back again at Lelan. Her mouth had dropped open!

We had arrived at a location that looked like a movie set, or at least a page from the lifestyles of the rich and famous. Enormous grounds surrounded an equally impressive rock structure that was Villa Ferraia.

Vittorio explained as we entered the patio that there were four pools of varying temperatures, an observatory for stargazing, horses, and hours for guests to enjoy walks and reflection. This was a passionate man who informed us that conversation and the sharing of cultures and ideas was why he and his family had restored Villa Ferraia. I was speechless!

Vittorio gave us a tour of the rooms, and I was struck that most were larger than my first apartment in Florence! Huge suites with oversized bathrooms and Jacuzzi tubs could have his guests forgetting this was Italy. The views of mountains and forests from every window lent to the isolated yet peaceful ambience of the property.

I was delighted at this man's generous invitation to show us the villa but suddenly felt shy about his expectations. Did he realize that I was just in the process of trying to organize my very first tour and not a seasoned businesswoman? Would he have offered to bring me here if he'd known that I was desperately hoping to get just ten women to attend one tour in April?

A young woman interrupted my thoughts and announced to Vittorio that it would be thirty minutes until lunch would be served. I thought this may be our cue to leave, so I asked Vittorio if he planned to take us back to Siena.

"Of course," he boomed in his loud voice. "Right after we all have a *beautiful* lunch together in the solarium!" Again, I made eye contact with Lelan, and this time, her eyes were twinkling. Neither of us could really believe this was happening!

Thirty-three

My girlfriends had left Italy and also left me with much higher spirits than before their arrival. While my apartment seemed extra quiet without my guests, I was learning more and more how to live alone, and enjoy it.

Meditation in the morning continued to be a constant source of peace in my life, and I studied the different light streaming through my windows from the gardens and my young neighbor, who delighted me. Occasionally, my neighbors would be chatting on the patio and the sound of their voices with the melodic Italian and laughter would remind me of my solitude.

I had never thought about a future that would include living alone. I'd always been happily surrounded by family and the demands of running a home. It seemed strange to be alone, day in and day out, but I was finding a rhythm of life that worked for me here.

The group of expats in Florence was a comfortable circle of friends to me now, and we took tours and had lunch together at least once a week. Pat was living in the Santa Croce neighborhood, and I would meet her on Ponte alle Grazie several times a week. Despite how little time we'd known each other, she was one of the few people that I felt totally myself around, and I teased her that her only fault was her love for tea over coffee.

At Vittorio's invitation, I asked several friends to join me in trying out Villa Ferraia for a few days. Expats don't tend to be shy, and most everyone said, enthusiastically, yes! A lively bunch of ladies—Angie, Susan, Mary, Anne, Pat, and I—boarded the train to Siena, where Vittorio met us. He had invited an astronomer to come up on a Saturday night and explain to us what we were seeing through his powerful telescope. I'd become quite spoiled with wonderful adventures, but this was truly something extraordinary.

I'd sent my first article to *Huffington Post* and titled it "The Decision." After a couple of back-and-forth emails with the link of how to submit my post, I was still waiting for it to be published. The reply email had said all submissions were published within twenty-four hours, but after two days I'd decided I had done something wrong. I hated to bother my editor yet again but wrote and asked her if she would check on why my article hadn't appeared.

I received a very quick response informing me that they liked the article so much they were saving it for a feature on Friday! I was too green to really understand what that meant, but a few published author friends informed me it was very good news!

Vittorio arrived at the train station in Siena to pick us up and explained what he had planned after lunch. None of us had seen the Abbey of San Galgano, now roofless, along with the Rotonda di Montesiepi, which houses the tomb of San Galgano with the sword stuck in the ground. Vittorio also wanted to take us by one of his friend's stores where olives were being pressed into olive oil that day. It sounded divine!

Lunch at the enormous dining room table was perfect, and the ladies were as impressed with the elegant surroundings as I had first been. We turned down *limoncello* after eating, so as to not opt for a nap instead of the trip with Vittorio.

As I headed to my room to get a jacket, I checked the *Huffington Post* "Post+50" section, and there it was! The title had been changed, a picture added, but it was my story on the top left corner! I was overcome with amazement at the placement and response the article was already receiving. I quickly posted the link on my Facebook and Twitter pages, and then, unable to erase the beautiful image in my head of my name on a *Huffington Post* article, joined the others for more adventures!

Thrilled about the new avenue for promoting my writing and the tour, I quickly submitted three more articles to *Huffington Post*. They continued to feature my work, and I received a lot of responses from people I knew—and didn't know. The daily education I received from life in Italy made it easy to share tips for travelers to Tuscany, and it also enriched my expat life. The writing flowed fairly easily and took me back to my years in school when I was always happier with an essay test rather than a multiple choice. Writing was cathartic for me those days, and after I would meditate each morning with a big cup of American coffee, I would sit down to write.

Justin finished up his work in Germany, came to visit me, and spent Thanksgiving with my friends. Angie and Doug had invited a group of us to their place in Impruneta for the holiday. While we were all doing some part of the preparation, Angie put her Italian landlady and now dear friend, Donatella, in charge of cooking the turkey.

Knowing my son would be here for Thanksgiving and then return again in December for Christmas made me think I could make it through the holiday season. It was generous on his part to make his plans around me and generous of my girl to say she was okay without us there. While I couldn't visualize how the season would look, and unfold, in Italy, I knew it was part of the experience. It would be different for all of us.

Thirty-four

Reinvention is an interesting word that others have often used about me, but I have purposefully not. I hadn't set out on a foreign makeover, but rather, just a new experience.

However, one morning I listened to one of my favorite teachers, Dr. Wayne Dyer, speak, and I wondered if I misjudged the power of reinventing.

The more you see yourself as what you'd like to become and act as if what you want is already there, the more you'll activate those dormant forces that will collaborate to transform your dream into your reality.

I had seen doors open to me that I had only dreamed of, and people seemed to have appeared in my life just at the perfect time. The business was attracting some interest as Sarah and I were spreading the message out to our circles, and I was amazed at the speed in which my new life was moving.

Alexandra and I had become great friends, and she had introduced me to many people of influence in Florence. The diverse and intellectual artists and scholars were fascinating to me, and learning more about Italian culture was an ongoing, daily field of study.

I felt grittier in a strong, self-reliant way. Jane may have had to catch the initial geckoes, but I tossed one out on the rooftop a few days after she left. I no longer let the predictable Italian swoopers butt in front of me at the post office, nor took the first "no" that anyone in the government offices offered.

It was the first time in my life that I hadn't had anyone or anything that could be seen as a parachute. I was on my own for the equal parts of excitement and fear that that sentence conjured up! There was no deep pocket, strong arm, or soft landing should I have fallen.

I had also become an observer of people and Italian culture. To be immersed in it in daily life was the only way to truly get a sense of the difference, the rhythm, and the cadence of a culture I had not been raised in.

I remember walking down via Calzaiuoli in the fall of 2012, looking in the store windows and eating a gelato. My hair had been freshly cut (not trimmed) by Oliver, my leggings and purse newly purchased. It was a Sunday afternoon, and the three-generation *passeggiata*, or walk, was in full swing.

I had the distinct feeling that someone was watching me, and looking up I met the full gaze of a gentleman leaning on a doorway of a clothing shop.

"How's your gelato?" he asked, in perfect English, with only a slight trace of an Italian accent. His head was tilted to one side, slight smile, definitely flirting.

I stopped dead in my tracks and just looked at him. I hadn't said a word, dressed head-to-toe in recent Italian purchases, and yet, somehow, he had pegged me as American.

How did he know?

I thought about that moment for a long time afterward. More than just a little mystified, I couldn't identify what had given my nationality away. Usually, it was my American accent, but this time I hadn't uttered a word. This man, who I came to know as Giacomo, had zeroed in on something else, *something* I didn't know was apparent, and he had no doubt where my homeland was.

I often think about that interaction, and I chuckle whenever I think of how perplexed I had been at his seeming superpowers! He had known I was American at fifty paces!

I have come to understand Giacomo's skill, and I have also come to know all too well Giacomo's flirting techniques.

Omnipresent in Florence, he was a consummate businessman who knew how to sell Italian clothing to American women! I have acquired some of Giacomo's superpowers, although not in flirting.

I can now pick out Americans on the bridge, walking toward me, long before I can see their faces. It's in their walk, the openness of their shoulders, the lift of their neck. It's in the open way they look around and scan the faces of those they pass. It isn't Italian, and it is obvious once you spend day in and day out in their culture.

Eye contact and full smiles that communicate friendliness, openness, and politeness in the U.S. have a different impact in Italy.

I read an article that said one cannot fully assimilate into another culture unless one begins prior to age five. I don't know if that is really true. I only know that I, too, can spot Americans when they walk into a restaurant or stand on a street corner. A bit too loud, too bossy, and too casual for the Italians, Americans can be easy to spot.

American tourists will often remark that the servers in restaurants or shop owners are unfriendly to them. I have come to know it's just a difference in approach, but it has taken time to understand. Italians are the warmest, kindest people I have ever known, as long as you know rules of behavior, the *bella figura*—Italian style.

I was unintentionally privy to a conversation next to me because two women were seated at a table less than six inches away from mine. I had come to a café named Rifrullo for a mid-afternoon espresso, hoping it would kick in and provide me with some needed energy to continue through my day without a nap.

The women were speaking in English, as they were American tourists, and each of them drank a cappuccino, which told me they weren't familiar with Italian culture. Cappuccino is a morning drink to Italians, who will check their watches if you order one later than ten a.m. It is never considered an appropriate drink after a meal, as it contains milk; gelato, apparently, is another story!

They were discussing their dinner last night at a local restaurant and how aloof the server was. I purposefully looked the other way and didn't want them to know I was American. These were the comments and dialogues that made me cringe.

The longer I live in Italy, the more I understand how little I understand. It takes a lifetime to fully assimilate into another culture and the rhythm of another culture, and there is no way to speed up the process.

While it's fine to be a tourist here and not know the local culture and customs, it's not right to criticize. These ladies described an evening that was perfectly acceptable to Italian customers. As tourists, they didn't know the cultural norms and became critical rather than curious about the differences.

As I sipped my coffee, my mind drifted back to a conversation I had with a man named Richard almost a decade before. He'd been a friend whom I'd met at the gym—a curmudgeon of sorts with a keen intellect and wicked tongue.

As he'd ridden the stationary bike one morning, I walked in and leaned against the handlebars. Off on some tangent that had me wound up, I'd spouted off all the injustice of the situation and how absolutely and completely in the right I was.

He'd waited until my rant was over and, wiping the perspiration from his brow with a full-sized towel, announced that there was more than one way to L.A.

"What the hell does that mean?" I'd asked.

"Well, Lisa," he said in a way I knew was going to end in a story, "let's say you and I were going to attend a conference in L.A. You, because you are you, would get on an early-morning flight, check into a lovely hotel and arrive at the conference the evening before it began."

"While I," he continued, "would load up my truck and set out a week prior. I'd camp at Zion and Bryce National Parks, stop to visit friends in Las Vegas, and roll into California just in time for the conference. I'd have taken time to enjoy the scenery, stop and eat when I wanted to, hike an unknown trail if I felt like it, and *then* I'd arrive in L.A."

"So," he asked me with his piercing blue eyes sparkling and wearing just a hint of a smile, "who won L.A.?"

"Who *won* L.A.?" I responded, unimpressed.

"Yes, who won?" he asked me again.

I shrugged, wishing I hadn't been caught in one of Richard's verbal riddles. I'd been on the receiving end of his steel trap of a brain before, and Richard didn't suffer foolish responses lightly.

"I don't think anyone *won* L.A.," I answered.

"That's right, Grasshopper," he said, with a flash of his brilliant smile. "Each person found their own way, no one way superior to another. Always remember, Lisa, there are many ways to get to L.A."

I thought of Richard so many times since I came to Italy. He had loved to travel to faraway places, to plop himself right smack in the middle of a new culture and situation and navigate his way out. He was the first one to teach me the concepts of Buddhism, which were so foreign to anything I'd ever learned. Most importantly, in his own ornery way, I knew he loved me.

Richard had a massive heart attack while swimming in a Utah lake, preparing for a triathlon a few years after that conversation. All the bike riding, vegan diet, and weight loss couldn't save him from his genetic programming. It broke my heart when I heard he was gone, mostly because I'd never dared tell him how dear he was to me.

He taught me a concept that I've never forgotten and use daily in my new country: there is more than one right way to do just about anything. Opening my heart and my mind has shown me again and again, Richard was spot on; there are many ways to L.A.

Somewhere, in the painted pastel sunset over Ponte Vecchio, I hope he hears me when I ask him if he's proud of me now…I think he would be.

"Thank you, Richard. I miss you."

Thirty-five

Thanksgiving Day had arrived, and so had my boy! Andrea Vignoli, Angie and Doug's landlord in Impruneta, came to pick up the six expats in a sparkling clean Mercedes van and drove us to their home. While it certainly didn't feel like the Thanksgivings I had known in the past, it was exciting to get outside of Florence to the small, rural community of Impruneta and share this day with friends from Italy, the U.K., and the U.S.

As we drove through the narrow roads, I marveled at the view of the olive groves, hills, and villas tucked in through the valley. The leaves on the grapevines and trees were changing colors, and Impruneta had a rustic, old charm about it that was very different from the bustle of Florence. Stone walls lined both sides of the road, and Andrea honked often to alert oncoming traffic as we wound our way through the Chianti valley.

Immediately upon arrival, Justin and I got to work on chopping vegetables, and, in typical Thanksgiving tradition, each of us had brought a dish to share. Angie and Doug were warm and inviting, the perfect hosts, and the long table was set and glistened in the late afternoon sunshine. I glanced over at my son and was filled with pride, admiration, and disbelief that we, somehow, were involved in this very unique gathering.

Donatella and Andrea were the last to formally arrive even though they had come just from the apartment below! Both carried platters brimming full of food and finally, the turkey. Donatella spoke very good English, and I immediately noticed her brown eyes were warm, friendly, and almost familiar. She and Angie had become such good friends, that the next month's parting already brought tears to their eyes when they mentioned it. A rare stroke of serendipity brought these two couples together, and it was obvious that they felt more like family than landlords and tenants.

Andrea spoke Spanish with Justin, as Andrea didn't speak much English. I watched his face, which was animated, and in typical Italian style his hands were flying in constant motion. He often looked to Donatella to clarify what was being said in English by the rest of the group, and while he was quiet, his energy was intelligent and kind. He'd talked about a new business venture he was to start as a driver. He would be working with an agency in Florence, but also on his own, and I thought to myself that this may be just who I was looking for to drive the tour groups to Cortona and Montepulciano.

Angie, Pat, and I were laughing about a trip we had taken the previous week to meet a woman Angie had been stalking! Angie had read Jennifer Criswell's book *At Least You're in Tuscany*, a memoir of the author's first year in the small town of Montepulciano, and wanted to meet her before she and Doug returned to the U.S. On a visit to the small town of Montepulciano, Angie had asked around where she might find Jennifer and was told to go to Poliziano winery where Jennifer worked.

Angie contacted Jennifer, and we arranged to meet her at the winery for a tour and a tasting. Jennifer was flattered, not the least bit afraid of her newest fans, and laughed that she had been so easy to find. Afterward, we had all returned to spend the night in Cortona and wander through its narrow streets, eat at La Grotta, and shop.

I immediately liked Jennifer Criswell, and after seeing the lush and expansive winery of Poliziano, I knew this was the experience I wanted my tour groups to have. Doors opened, and people appeared in perfect timing! It seemed to happen almost daily!

We took our seats at the table and held hands while Doug said a Thanksgiving prayer. My heart was full of an array of emotions that day. I was grateful for friends who understood, as no one else could, what it was like to live in a foreign country. I was grateful for my friends and family on the other side of the world, who were celebrating a traditional Thanksgiving Day, but my heart ached with missing my daughter.

As our day wound down, we left as one usually does from an Italian home—with gifts and freshly made food. It was olive oil that day from the trees just outside of Donatella and Andrea's home, pressed in the community's co-op. New olive oil, green and peppery, is absolutely exquisite! I realized, as I juggled leftovers and cans of olive oil in my arms, that I had been spoiled forever by the food of Tuscany.

The night air was crisp and chilly, and as I walked, Donatella caught up to me and linked her arm through mine. She told me how much she enjoyed our meeting and asked if she could call when she came into Florence. "Could you find time to meet for lunch or shopping?" she asked me. I stopped to look at her and said of course we could get together. Both she and Andrea seemed like my friends already, and I looked forward to being with them again.

The half-hour drive back to Florence was much quieter than the drive to Impruneta had been, as we each drifted in our own thoughts and took short naps. The sun had set, and the long stream of car lights into the city looked endless. I thought about love, and family, and friends who felt like family, and all the Thanksgivings that I'd spent. I had never pictured the holiday happening any other way than it had for all those years in Utah, and yet my heart was full of happiness for the day Justin and I had spent. It felt so comforting to have him next to me—a part of my former life sharing my new one.

I thought about the nature of love, the concept that something intangible is so real. I've heard it said that love never dies, that it just changes forms. I'm not sure about that. What I do know is the love I gave in the past was real. And I would like to believe that the love I received was real as well. The fact that it didn't stay the same, or ended with betrayal wasn't something I cared to hold on to any longer. For that, I was thankful.

Thirty-six

A damp cold settled in Florence during December, and Justin left for a few weeks of climbing in the Dolomites. I paid for his airfare there, as his Christmas gift, and would be sending a few things home with him for Lauren. Other than a couple of small gifts exchanged ahead of time with friends, I did no shopping, no wrapping, and no decorating for the holidays.

Each main street in Florence was decorated with lights and a unique theme, from stars to twinkling bicycles, and store windows and shops were tastefully readied for the holiday. It was all very low-key, classic, and beautiful—what one would expect in the fashion of Florence!

I worried that the actual day would be difficult for me, but the time leading up to Christmas felt good. It felt healing, and there was a freedom in not having all the holiday preparations to do.

I had no desire to be in Utah or the United States. Just the thought of the endless Christmas carols and over-the-top buying and decorating made me feel a little sick. Simple and elegant suited my mood fine, and hearing no Christmas carols was a gift in itself! Still raw and fresh were the wounds of a family splitting apart and life as I had known it dissolving. I was content to be half a world away.

One afternoon, Pat called to see if I had seen the lights on the other side of Ponte Vecchio, heading toward Palazzo Pitti. When I said I had not, she ordered me to bundle up, and she would call for me as soon as darkness had settled in Florence. Arm in arm, we strolled along the streets, now bare of tourists, and marveled at the festive feel of our town. Stopping for *aperitivo*, we ended up having several glasses of wine each and sharing our stories and our souls with each other. I could trust Pat and knew that about our friendship. She was rock solid, and I thanked the heavens that she was staying for Christmas in Italy as well.

Twilight in Florence paints the sky a color that I had never seen before. Deep indigo eventually turns to black, but initially it lingers long after the moon is up. While my days were busy planning the tour and writing, nighttime crept in with full-blown anxiety.

It had abated while Justin shared the apartment; knowing someone I loved was sleeping under the same roof as me felt so comforting. But now, each night as I turned the bedcovers, my heart raced. Feeling utterly alone in the world, I was overwhelmed with panic for just a few minutes.

This was new to me, and I was doing my best to honor the feelings while keeping my wits about me. It wasn't an unseen intruder or ghost haunting these ancient walls that unnerved me, but rather the feeling of drowning in my aloneness.

I was utterly alone in a way I never anticipated or desired. I knew my life was filled with miracles and delights, but right around eleven at night, this unwanted intruder crept into my apartment and permeated my soul with loneliness.

"Just get in bed, Lisa" is something I said aloud every night that I was in Florence for the past two years. I don't know when it stopped, but at some point, like all endless nights that turn to day, it lifted.

Thirty-seven

Learning a foreign language is a humbling experience, as there is always a certain amount of embarrassment that is going to result. By this time, I didn't have the "deer in the headlights" reaction that I did the first year, ending with me completely tongue-tied and silent, but regardless of how much I practiced, it never was as easy in real life as it was when I was alone in my apartment.

Equally confusing to me was the metric system of measurement. Just when I was brave enough to try again, I ordered *ragù* sauce from the deli at the market only to have the surrounding crowd burst out in laughter. As one Italian grandma pointed out to me in Italian, I had just ordered enough for everyone in the whole market!

I was getting daily experience in letting go of other people's opinions of me—one of Wayne Dyer's common themes—and learning not to care much. Part of the comfort may have resulted from knowing I never had to see any of these people again, and part of me just knew how much sheer will and determination it took every day to live here.

"I'm just a girl from East Millcreek in Salt Lake City," I'd mumble to myself, "and a housewife from Sandy." I certainly had never prepared myself for navigating the open market of Sant'Ambrogio or to fight for my space in line at the *fruttivendolo*'s stand. I knew I had to keep trying to assimilate into my new neighborhood, speak Italian, and anything I learned was better than not speaking the language at all.

Once, however, while staying at Villa Ferraia, I'd announced to the mostly Italian guests seated at the long table that I'd be going upstairs after that delicious lunch for a little nap. However, I said *pistolino* instead of *pisolino*, which meant I'd be retiring for a little penis. At those times I learned a valuable lesson, which was: it's better to own a mistake and be self-deprecating than try to fake it!

Suffice it to say, I never have mentioned taking a nap since.

I do know that any effort I spent learning Italian was reciprocated a thousand times over. Italian is only spoken in Italy, and while I've heard that the French are not so appreciative of hearing their language botched and contorted, Italians warmed to me immediately just for trying! If I would ask them for clarification on the pronunciation, or what something was called in Italian, they would graciously and happily assist me.

My walk back to San Niccolò over Ponte alle Grazie would find me practicing the new words I learned and rehearsing what I should have said, what I would say next time.

Shopping at the market was a daily event, so I had lots of practice. Given that the produce was so fresh, unprocessed, and hadn't been sprayed to last for weeks, as well as the fact that my apartment was fifty-six steps straight up, I kept just a day's worth of groceries in my kitchen.

For most of the hours of the day, I loved the sound of the Italian language. I adored the melodic cadence and emotion in phrases, and the passion with which words were shared. Only at night, when my brain was tired, would I hear the neighbors talking through the open window and think, "Can't we all just speak English, just for a few minutes?"

Thirty-eight

Justin returned to Florence for Christmas just as the Internet in the apartment went out. Despite numerous calls to the rental agency, no Internet resumed for the week before Christmas. I knew it wasn't their fault, and Adriana was contacting Telecom in my behalf, but I also knew that the Internet being out for a week or more wasn't unusual in Italy.

Justin and I headed to Rifrullo for coffee each morning, and to read our emails on the computers there, but so much work was going undone on my part. Most of all, I needed to be in contact with Lauren via Skype, and as Christmas Day approached I worried that wouldn't happen.

While Justin and I had plans for dinner with friends on Christmas Day, I needed to find a place for us to stay where we could have easy access to Wi-Fi and Skype with my girl. Her work schedule was such that she had only Christmas Day off, and it was imperative to me that we include her in our day.

Most of the hotels in Cortona were closed for the winter, but I researched until I found that Hotel Italia would be open. I booked one of the last rooms they had, and Justin and I packed a bag and caught the train for my favorite town, Cortona.

If Florence was beautifully decorated for Christmas, Cortona was magical! Cortona has just one main street, via Nazionale, which is still called Rugapiana by the older locals. It dead ends into the main square where the steps leading to town hall make for easy gathering. A huge tree was decorated and each store was festive in the way that I imagine has been the same for decades. Boughs of green and twinkling lights framed each store, and a huge sled filled with packages filled the large window of the antique store. It was enchanting, and I found my spirit always was lifted by a visit to Cortona.

Mariano met us at the station and agreed to drive us to Montepulciano, with a stop at the Poliziano winery for a tasting. In writing to Jennifer, she said the winery was actually closed, but a man named Fabio would meet us for a quick, private tasting. He was gracious and kind beyond belief as he provided a private tour for us to see the Carlotti family's Poliziano winery and fall in love with their Asinone wine. It was a rare experience to wander the wine cellar in absolute stillness and have the entire estate to ourselves!

Montepulciano and Cortona are famous for the spectacular views across the Tuscan countryside. This season, however, and particularly on that day, the fog and mist had rolled in, blanketing the view. A cold hush seemed to have settled over Montepulciano, and an eerie atmosphere was in sharp contrast to its summertime feel.

Christmas Eve in the piazza was filled with Cortona locals, with benches warmed by the same men who sat there each afternoon and a brass band playing Christmas carols. I am pretty sure anyone and everyone who played a brass instrument in the small town was included in the group! What it lacked in quality was completely made up for in the heart of the marching band. We watched as they circled the small piazza in the misty cold air, playing the familiar songs of the season. Later we ate dinner in a cozy *trattoria* while a fire blazed in the corner, and my heart was filled with gratitude that I wasn't there alone.

After breakfast on Christmas morning, we found Teuscher's café open and busy. I was amazed! I had no idea stores would be operating as usual and people would be out and about. The entire community was bustling to and from church, homes, and the cafés. Justin and I watched a passing parade from a bench outside of La Grotta as *Buon Natale* rang repeatedly from one side of the square to the other. I felt very much the observer—the outsider—but not in a lonely way. I was at home here in a way that made no sense to anyone but me.

The previous January I had sworn in my best Scarlett O'Hara manner that, with God as my witness, I would never scrape off a car windshield again! And here I didn't have to do that. Of course, in Florence I didn't own a car, but I did freeze daily.

I kept my down coat on even inside the apartment and typed with fingerless gloves. While the city of Florence regulates the hours heat can be on, it also makes using it dreadfully expensive. Having paid almost four hundred dollars the previous month for utilities, I dutifully minimized consumption, but I was cold.

Daily, walking across the Ponte alle Grazie bridge would chill me to the bone. I gave in, finally, and bought a *scaldasono*, which is the Italian version of a large heating pad. As I explained to the saleswoman that I didn't need the double mattress size, just the single, she replied, "*Signora, da sola?*" (Are you alone/single?)

This question was always accompanied by a worried expression, regardless of my response, so I'd learned to just nod.

The Signora is indeed *"da sola,"* and freezing!

Thirty-nine

La bella figura

While the government seems woefully inept at processing anything in a timely or efficient manner, the rest of life in Italy fascinated me. It is a country that seems more concerned about making a good impression than having a robust economy, and no Florentine woman would take the garbage out without matching shoes and handbag.

The longer I was here, the more I was aware of the subtleties of creating *la bella figura*—roughly translated to be a good impression.

The casual way of Americans, eagerly friendly and without a language that differentiates between formal and informal, is not the way of Italians. While books and blogs are solely devoted to the concept of *la bella figura* (or its counterpart, *la brutta figura*), one must really spend time here to start to grasp its significance.

There are rules about behavior, manners, and dress that one is expected to know and follow. While there seems to be no rules on the road nor orderliness to any bureaucratic system, *la bella figura* reigns supreme in all interactions with Italians. Knowing this, and knowing I wanted to create a business here, I observed a lot and learned.

As a foreigner, I noticed how polished everyone seemed to be—from their shoes to their greetings—it was staggering!

Confident and manicured, constantly aware of aesthetic beauty, Italians seem to be a walking advertisement for the good life.

But the rules extend beyond dress, and that's where it gets a bit tricky. I wasn't raised here, I didn't know the rules; like many ambiguous but understood concepts, they aren't easily explained. I could tell that it takes time in this culture to even begin to understand it, and there is no faking.

Some of my lessons have come about via withering looks from the *fruttivendolo*, the server at a *trattoria*, or (God forbid) an Italian grandma at the market! The older women seem to rule the markets and, if provoked, they think nothing of leaning over to slap a hand that is touching the produce without the requisite plastic glove.

Don't share food, even pizza, or drink cappuccino after breakfast. Each pasta has a correct sauce that accompanies it, and every shop owner should be greeted as one enters and exits their store. Those are the easy ones.

But, true to all things Italian, there exists a certain paradox in *la bella figura*. For instance, despite all the formality with greetings and politeness, Italians are notorious for butting in line or refusing to move an inch on the sidewalk to allow others to pass by. They are dreadful on the highways and rarely pick up after their dogs. Some days this would amuse me, and other days, make me crazy.

Because of the complexities of navigating through this new culture, my second year taught me the art of the pause.

I'd never been one to pause before speaking up, questioning, or moving forward. It's very American to forge ahead! But that doesn't sit well within the culture here, and I learned that pausing and observing were great teachers.

As I lined up the day tours, hotels, restaurants, and experiences for the tour group arriving in April, I closely observed the Italians I interacted with. Often, just taking a moment's pause gave me the added information I needed on how to respond.

I have learned that email and phone contact is less effective than meeting face to face; and a face-to-face meeting must always include a sit-down with a coffee. I learned to slow down, as rushing translates to classic American impatience, and be profusely gracious. This is a society that still places a lot of weight on manners, and I learned quickly that working on *la bella figura* was the only way to flourish in Florence.

Doors continued to open for me throughout Tuscany, and the graciousness and gratitude I felt for those I was doing business with was genuine. I was carving out the structure of the tour and felt confident that we could provide a remarkable experience for American women. And I was working daily to improve on my own *bella figura.*

Forty

Wouldn't it be wonderful if every woman could give herself the gift of getting away from all her daily responsibilities just to spend time in quiet reflection? The answers to my own heart's desires could only be found in the silence I'd created in a small apartment overlooking the Bardini Garden. So far away from the reach of my American life, I turned inward and started cultivating a peace that had eluded me in previous years.

I'd let go of so much on a physical level, but now I found myself letting go of other less tangible things. I let go of a lot of expectations. Nowhere in my adult years had I dreamed of living alone, in a foreign country without any income! Yet here I was doing just that and finding a deep satisfaction in my days.

As the new year arrived, I reflected on all I'd let go in 2013 and all those who had let go of me.

Living in a foreign country had taught me, on a daily basis, that we each see our world through the lens of our own culture and experiences. Every story is real to the person telling it, beliefs are thoughts we've had many times, and arguing about who is right rarely solves any disagreement.

Maybe I was just tired of the fight, of justifying my side or hurting over those who had stopped loving me, but 2013 found me not caring so much about my past. Living in anonymity, among people who had no expectations of me, had given me total freedom to create a new life, and that's what I had done. While lonely at times, I was becoming my own best friend, comfortable in my own skin with my own thoughts. Best of all, I was finally at peace.

By releasing most of my fears, joy found an easier route into my heart. Repeated visits to the Questura for bureaucratic issues had toughened me up enormously, as had the Italian *nonne* in the markets. Happily I crossed the expansive piazzas, almost empty in the winter cold, and I marveled at the chance to pause and take in the views.

I didn't watch any television and found I listened to music less than I had before, preferring times of silence in each day. Now a stranger to new American culture, TV, movies, or music, I found I didn't miss them. Occasionally a headline would come across my MSN news feed alerting me that someone I didn't recognize had just broken up with someone else I didn't recognize, and I was happily ignorant of all of it!

Lastly, I let go of future expectations. I made no New Year's resolutions, thinking I would simply try to do the best I could each day. If the past couple of years taught me anything, they taught me that I have no idea what's ahead! I visualized goals and planned for the tours, but I left most of my future without expectations. A big "we'll see" became my motto as the cold, damp days of winter settled into my beloved city.

Forty-one

Once you make a decision, the Universe conspires to make it happen.

—Ralph Waldo Emerson

As the days became warmer, my spirit became lighter. Doors were opening, plans coming to fruition, and the inaugural tour for women was going to happen in April.

I learned the key to doing business in Italy was to slow down and always have time for a coffee. Emails and phone calls were the efficient business modality of the United States, but not in Italy. Jumping into the straightforward communication about business details, while common in the U.S., was not appreciated here. When I spoke with managers of hotels and restaurants, they generally preferred face to face conversation.

Hotel Pierre was my choice for the ladies' accommodations. It is located just a block from Piazza della Repubblica, smack-dab in the action but amazingly quiet. A favorite among Italian guests, its stately wooden fixtures seemed to match the Gothic and magical atmosphere of the city. Just a few minutes' walk to the Uffizi Gallery or the Duomo, I felt the ladies would easily be able to find their way "home." However, it was the easy charm and kindness of the hotel's director, Fabrizio Pacciani, that convinced me to put my signature on the dotted line!

As I organized each day's itinerary, I chose the best of the best of what I had done here. I wanted the ladies to experience not only the sites all visitors to Florence see but also meet locals and artists and eat at smaller *trattorias*, which the average tourist wouldn't find.

While I had had some real doubts about the tour filling, in the end there were ten women who were on their way to Tuscany to spend eight days and seven nights. Several were adding a couple of extra nights after the tour to stay at Villa Ferraia. It was a big responsibility, but I couldn't wait!

Andrea and I had spent time communicating, in English and Italian, and came to the conclusion that we spoke on a toddler level. We could get our message across, but we frequently didn't do so with full sentences! I loved being with Andrea for language time, as it never felt intimidating to ask (for the twentieth time) how to phrase something.

He would be our driver, and that gave me a huge sense of comfort. I knew Andrea was reliable (and he'd have to answer to Donatella if anything went wrong), and I was so at ease with both of them. Through the months, we had spent many meals and conversations until now they seemed like my Italian family.

The week before the ladies were to arrive for the tour, I felt not only excitement but a great sense of responsibility. For many, this was their first trip to Italy. I wanted to be sure that they enjoyed each minute and knew how precious both their time and money were.

I reviewed the hotel lists, accommodations, extra nights, and transportation dates and times until I could repeat them in my sleep. I wanted everything to go off without a hitch, and most of all, I hoped they would feel the magic touch of Tuscany.

Forty-two

Loving ourselves through the process of owning our own story is the bravest thing we will ever do.
—Brene Brown

The new business of taking women through Tuscany culminated in April 2013, as ten women joined Sarah and me for the inaugural tour. Each woman either knew one of us or knew someone who did! I understood fully that it was a big financial commitment, and they were placing a great deal of trust in my meeting them in Florence. Much like I had been before seeing Lorenzo's face upon my arrival here, I'm sure they also had a little apprehension!

The part that couldn't be planned in advance, of course, was the sharing that would make travelers into friends and experiences into treasured memories. As we told our personal stories over dinners, hikes, wine tastings, and shopping for leather goods, the group quickly blended.

The last night of the tour, I led a class that I called "Courage, Passion, and Joy." I told them of my coming to Italy and finally to Cortona, where I had understood that my purpose here was to honestly and openly share my story. I hadn't opened up a lot with others in the past two years, and it was touching to see the understanding in their eyes. I had the overwhelming sensation that one person's courage gives rise to others believing they could do the same. I felt deeply satisfied that there was a purpose in this business beyond just the sightseeing in Tuscany. Life is supposed to be joyful—I believed that with all my heart, and I wanted to share that belief with other women!

Huffington Post continued to feature the biweekly articles I sent in, and I received many emails from readers and travelers alike. Often, someone would write to say they were visiting Florence and would ask me to meet them for a coffee or *aperitivo*. I was amazed at the vast array of travelers, writers, photographers, and friends whose lives intersected mine in this foreign country. The openness and friendliness of travelers has been a source of constant amazement and joy to me. The privilege of meeting so many strangers wasn't lost on this middle-aged woman from Utah who had never dreamed of living her life anywhere else! Telling my story was a process I was learning to understand. I didn't share it all, but I could see that it was serving as an inspiration to others thinking about their own leap of faith, and for that I was grateful.

I continued to be drawn to Cortona. Every other weekend, at least, would find me taking the eighty-two-minute train ride from Florence to this tiny town perched on a hill. Often with a friend, but sometimes alone, I would walk the main street of via Nazionale to shop, have a coffee at Teuscher's, or enjoy a medieval festival in the piazzas. Cortona's temperature was cooler compared to that of Florence in the hot summer months, and the locals were inviting and friendly.

The unofficial mayor of Cortona, Ivan Botanici, became a good friend and business associate. Ivan was everything an American woman dreams of in an Italian man. Well over six feet tall, he was taller than most Italian men, usually wearing his signature crisply ironed long-sleeve shirt and jeans, with his long hair pulled back in a man-bun. His good looks were eclipsed only by his natural charisma and Italian charm, and I never saw him not be the epitome of a fabulous host.

Ivan would not only prepare *aperitivo*—including his own olive oil, focaccia, paté, and prosecco—for the ladies but give them the history of Cortona. As he led them on a tour through his gorgeous art gallery, Galleria Il Pozzo, few could resist the photographs of Tuscany.

I felt fortunate to come to know him as a dear friend, and that summer I stayed in an apartment for two weeks that his wife's family owned. He gave me advice on where to stay in Cortona and how to fine-tune the details of my tours there. I smile at the serendipity that led me wandering into Cortona and, eventually, his gallery.

Forty-three

Dante Alighieri was one of Florence's native sons, although he was exiled to Ravenna, where he actually died and is buried. Despite the annual plea from the Mayor of Florence to have his remains returned to Santa Croce where a crypt is waiting, and where his statue stands guard outside, Ravenna's answer has always been a definite no. You didn't want him in life; you don't get him in death…or something to that effect.

All I know is, he must have written "Inferno" with Florence in the summertime in mind. Surely even hell could not be hotter!

As the humidity and the temperature both reached about ninety-five, I decided I was wilting and in need of a change. There was no air-conditioning in my San Niccolò apartment, and even those apartments equipped with it weren't sufficiently cooled. Opening the windows early in the morning proved to be futile, as no air was moving, and the only way to block the intense sun was to close the heavy green shutters. That was actually a good thing, as I had given up wearing clothing inside the apartment and placed ice packs on my head as I typed on the computer. I warned anyone who wished to Skype with me that they needed to send an email first so I could get dressed!

As the oppressive heat, humidity, and crowds of tourists descended on my beloved city, I looked for an escape. Cortona would provide two weeks' escape later in the summer, but I needed some relief sooner rather than later—and then

I remembered a beach house Lorenzo owned and had offered to me previously.

Lorenzo had been on my mind lately, and I missed him. We'd met for a coffee and lunch on occasion, but it was different now that I wasn't renting one of his apartments, and I missed him casually dropping by to tell me a story, ask for an English lesson, or bring me some fresh produce.

I loved living in San Niccolò, but it was a long walk to Hotel Pierre, where the ladies would stay during the next tours, and the apartment was expensive. I had needed the help of the staff at the apartment agency, Tuscan Feeling, when I was applying for my *Permesso di soggiorno*, but I wondered if I should renew my contract in September for another year.

Tuscan Feeling required another deposit equal to one month's rent to resign the contract, and Lorenzo had always forgone any finder's fee with me. I decided I'd send him an email asking about renting the beach house for a week and about a long-term apartment for next year. After I sent the email, I walked to the window to gaze out at the sun setting over Bardini Garden. This apartment was truly peaceful, and I felt comfortable in the neighborhood. The couple who owned the small Panino & Vino just down the street knew my usual order, and my lunch always came with a side of advice (usually regarding my love life) from Francesca and Dominic. Enzo always had a glass of prosecco waiting for me at BevoVino, and I knew I would miss the familiarity of this area if I moved.

As usual, when I couldn't come up with a decision, I put it out to the Universe to answer and asked for a sign.

Lorenzo had said I could indeed use his beach house in Monte Argentario, and to bring a friend along, but I had to be flexible on the dates and be ready to go with short notice. He'd squeeze me in between the summer's guests and let me know if there was a cancellation. A couple of days later, he called to see if I could leave on Saturday; I could stay for a week.

I called Pat, my dear English pal, who was one of the few people I knew I could hang with for a solid week. Pat was easy to be around: she loved to read, as I do, and was comfortable with an uncertain plan, as this was shaping up to be. We'd take the train, then have Lorenzo's friend pick us up and drive us to the house.

Of course, the first question Pat asked me was one I had asked Lorenzo. How much would it cost us? Lorenzo had given me the typical Italian shoulder shrug and deflected a question about money. Italians are never comfortable talking about an exact amount; Americans and Italians have very different relationships with money. We Americans talk about it—they don't.

When I told Pat that Lorenzo wouldn't give me an exact amount, she hesitated. Understandably she was concerned the excursion would be much more than she'd anticipated or budgeted for, but I just shrugged. All I knew was that Lorenzo was always generous and kind to me, and I didn't think he would gouge us in any way, but I'd asked three times with no luck on receiving an answer. "Don't worry," he would say and be off to another subject.

After a little more discussion, Pat and I agreed to go regardless of the cost. We didn't know what the accommodations would be, but we were desperate to escape the heat and the crowds of Florence. When Lorenzo had shown me the pictures of the beach house overlooking the crystal-blue water of the Mediterranean Sea, it was all the prodding I needed to pack my bags.

Forty-four

The night before Pat and I left for Monte Argentario had been a goodbye party for a friend. We met for a typical Italian dinner, which meant lots of courses, lots to drink, and a late night. When I finally walked into my apartment, I thought I heard a scratching noise, but I sleepily made the coffee for the next morning and crashed into bed.

It wasn't difficult to pack for a week at the beach house. Lorenzo had said the house was fully furnished, and Eduardo, our driver, would let us stop in Porto Santo Stefano, the main town, for groceries. I figured a few sundresses, shorts, and a swimsuit were about all I'd need. As I finished packing, I kept thinking I heard a noise, so I slowly inched my way toward the kitchen, where it seemed to originate.

Before I'd taken more than a few steps, there was no mistake. A full-on clatter of metal scratching against metal was occurring in the kitchen, and the only question I had was what was causing it. Horribly afraid of anything that moves faster than I do, I shuddered to think of what I might find if I turned the corner to look inside the compact kitchen.

I paused just outside the kitchen door as the noise stopped—and then my toes curled as it began again. I grabbed a heavy book off the shelf in the guest room and, with a heave, slammed it down on the floor by the kitchen.

A bird flew directly out of the kitchen and into the closed

window in the hall. Frantically, it began flying around the apartment as I flew (equally fast) out the front door!

My next-door neighbor had never really warmed up to me. I'd waved one time, when I had seen him out on his large, terra-cotta patio, but he had made it clear that American friendliness was not really to his liking. So I hesitated for a moment as I stood outside his door, wishing the third level had someone else living on it that I could ask for help.

As the unfriendly Italian man next door was my only option, I rang the doorbell and quickly knocked, trying to calm down and think of the Italian words for "There's a bird in my house! Will you help me?"

After a pause, I rang again and added another forceful knock when a gentleman opened the door. He was not the neighbor I had seen there before, but was holding a dust towel—clearly the housekeeper. Even in my frantic state, I couldn't help but notice the gorgeous furnishings that filled this apartment, just over his shoulder, complete with enormous paintings and oriental rugs.

As I blurted out my jumbled plea for help, I didn't give him much of a chance to decline. He walked into my apartment and opened up all the windows. As the bird flew from him, I crouched in the hallway between our apartments. Only once, when the bird flew toward me, did I shriek, but that was enough. His eyes told me that he'd decided I was out of my mind, but he continued to gently try to move the bird outside. Finally, he succeeded.

I tried to thank him, profusely, but he seemed more interested in getting back inside my neighbor's apartment, safely behind a locked door. I understood. I would have done the same thing.

I grabbed my suitcase, locked my apartment door, and hurried out to meet Pat for a week at the beach.

Eduardo met us, and as we climbed into the back of his tiny car, I wondered (as I always did) how it was I had become so trusting of strangers. The conversation between the three of us jumped from Italian to English, punctuated with a lot of laughter! Eduardo let us know that everything, including the grocery store, would close down for three hours in the afternoon, so we needed to stop in the town before we got to the beach house.

The grocery store was tiny, and while it had fresh produce, lots of fish, and a few basic items, it didn't offer an array of options. Pat was thrilled to find Weetabix for her morning breakfast, and although I'd never heard of it, I agreed to share it with her as well. We loaded up just enough to get us through a couple of days and met Eduardo back at the car.

Porto Santo Stefano looked like a charming seaside town, with pastel-colored restaurants lined up on the water. Pat and I decided we would come down here to spend a full day during the week, so we asked Eduardo when he could come to get us. Arranging a time and day, we started up the winding road lined with trees until we could look over the crystal-blue water with its sailboats. Everything about Porto Santo Stefano was different than Florence, and I was eager to see where we would call home for a week.

As we drove slowly down a private lane, I asked Eduardo if we were safe here. He assured us the most danger we'd encounter would be from the mosquitoes, maybe a snake! He pointed out a restaurant and beach within walking distance of the condo should we want to go out for dinner. As he dialed in the code, the gate opened and we drove through to find a peach-colored stucco home nestled among wildflowers, vines, trees, and rocks. Pat and I exchanged glances that said, *If the inside looks anything like the outside, we are in for a luxurious week!*

We thanked Eduardo and said goodbye, then headed inside to check out our accommodations for a week.

We set down the groceries and our small pieces of luggage, and I looked around at the spacious kitchen and dining area. Two master suites had sliding doors which took up the seaward side of the bedrooms. We quickly chose our rooms, dropped our luggage, and walked out onto the wraparound deck.

And then we both burst out laughing!

The deck looked over the Tyrrhenian Sea, with water so crystal clear and blue that it didn't seem real. Boats dotted the sea, and cliffs surrounded the water. There were no other homes in front of us, as this was truly beachfront property. The whole villa and view were like something out of a movie set.

Investigating further, we followed a flight of steps up to a rooftop patio, where lounges waited for us and the heady aroma of flowers scented the air. The property was filled with trees and vines, and the jungle-like plants hid any nearby homes. Seemingly alone on this gorgeous island, we watched as a small boat carved a path toward the shore. *Paradiso*!

Forty-five

The week at Lorenzo's beach house villa was one of the most memorable of my life. Pat and I pulled up maps to discover we were on the farthest northern tip of Monte Argentario. The rocky cliffs below us gave way to the water, which mesmerized us both for hours.

Seated on the deck, both in our white spa robes, we spotted Giglio and Giannutri Islands, as well as the mysterious island of Montecristo and the mountains of Corsica.

Pat's fondness for Weetabix was the only difference of opinion we had that week. Our mutual love of reading, walking, hiking, and just watching the water filled our days. We spent hours talking, and hours not talking, with equal comfort. Neither of us knew what was ahead that summer, and for both of us, it would be life changing. During those days, discovering a beautiful Vermentino wine and the joy of yoga on the rooftop deck superseded all else.

At night, we climbed the stairs to the rooftop with blankets to lie flat on our backs under the brilliant starlit sky. I was reminded of the summer nights I had spent, all through my youth, sleeping outside. Pat was amazed at my ability to point out the constellations, and I couldn't imagine a childhood that didn't include knowing such things! These stars seemed closer than any I could remember, however, and I felt we could reach up and bring one down to light our way back inside.

Pat told me stories of her beloved husband, Brian, who had passed away from cancer just a few years before. She described him in such detail that I felt I knew him too, and she told me of the place he was buried and how she knew she'd be buried right next to him. I thought about the comfort it must bring to know where you will ultimately be. She is a remarkable woman of intellect and courage, packed in a tiny stature with sparkling blue eyes and curly blonde hair, and I trusted her with my story as well.

We had just returned to sizzling hot Florence when Pat received a call from her son that she was needed at home in England. She began to pack that very day, and we said our hurried goodbyes. I took some of her things to store for her and fought back a few tears. Pat was never one for emails or Facebook, so I knew we wouldn't keep in close touch, but I also knew that we would be lifelong friends, the sort that pick up right where they left off.

I met with Lorenzo to find out what our week away had cost and if he had an apartment for me for the next year.

Lorenzo was uncomfortable jumping right into money business, so we did the usual small talk over a coffee, and I expressed repeatedly how much Pat and I had enjoyed the beach house. I could tell that truly pleased him, and, smiling, he finally gave me a price.

My first landlord and friend in Florence, Lorenzo, charged us little more than the cost of utilities for the week. He was always generous and caring toward me, and when he added that he had an apartment with a year's lease for me beginning in September, I said yes without even seeing it!

The new apartment was on via di Mezzo, close to the Sant'Ambrogio market where I liked to shop, closer to the center of town, but still in a neighborhood where there wouldn't be a lot of tourists. I knew it would be perfect.

The initial tour of Tuscany had been a success, I thought, and the ten ladies who booked the trip seemed to agree. Their testimonials expressed sincere appreciation at seeing Italy through a local's view, and the camaraderie that we all hoped would happen, did indeed. At our last night's dinner together, they gave me a journal with the inscription, "I'm in love with places I've never been to, and people I've never met." They had each written on a page, as have each one of the tours since then. The book is one of my most treasured possessions.

The biggest question ahead was how to get the word out about the tours. While these ten women were enthusiastic supporters, I wished for more than just word-of-mouth advertising. However, most avenues were very expensive, and as I researched them, I was amazed at the quantity of travel options in Tuscany. Even what I thought was a niche market—small groups just for women—was saturated. I was thankful I hadn't been this informed before we launched the first tour—I might not have dared!

Writing for *Huffington Post* brought credibility, but I wasn't certain it would translate to actual customers. Women's online resources had a plethora of travel companies and travel options to Italy. The first tours had run at just about break-even cost, and I was amazed to see the wide range of prices for similar tours.

Social media became the best way to spread the word without spending big bucks on advertising, so I dove into all fronts and reached out to offer a blog post or interview to anyone interested. While once I had been led (kicking and screaming) into the world of email, I now was curious about, and even embracing, all avenues of social media and exposure. It was incredible to think that I could sit alone in my apartment in Florence, Italy, and reach out across the world!

Forty-six

June 2014

Waking up alone on my birthday in Verona was planned, but it still felt odd. I'd decided to leave Florence for a couple of days and give myself the birthday present of going someplace new in Italy. I heard Verona was beautiful and would certainly be a bit cooler than Florence was at the end of June.

Verona was about a two-hour train ride, and I looked forward to going by myself. I liked nothing better than arriving in an Italian city and getting a bit lost. Wandering without a plan is heaven to me, and being able to meander and stop anywhere for any amount of time is really a solitary activity.

I took a taxi from the train station to the bed and breakfast I'd found online, but I now wished I'd chosen something closer to the city. I was out too far to walk into town, but the setting was serenely rural and relaxing.

In speaking with the young man at the front desk, I found out there was a bus stop just across the street where a bus came by hourly on its way into central Verona. Well, I knew this was still Italy, so the time and reliability were not exactly etched in stone. I unpacked my small suitcase and headed across the street to wait for the bus's arrival.

A friendly driver opened the door, and I pointed to the map as to where I wanted to exit. About twenty minutes later, he told me I was there and dropped me off by the Castelvecchio with its adjoining bridge. Built in a Gothic style with red bricks, it is powerful and imposing. I continued through Verona to see the bustling Piazza dei Signori and the amphitheater built in the first century that looks very much like the Colosseum in Rome. Of course, no visit to Verona would be complete without seeing the home and balcony of Shakespeare's Juliet, Casa di Giulietta. Love letters were posted all over the walls, and while touristy and certainly not her authentic house, it was sweet to visit.

The best part of the afternoon was the unexpected beauty I witnessed as I walked along the Adige River and took in the remarkably different feel to this city than Florence. The northern influence from Austria was evident in its design and architecture, and the restaurants I found were hidden in small walkways between buildings, covered with stones and wildflowers.

As I ate my lunch alone, I wondered when it was that I had crossed over from being uncomfortable eating alone to totally fine. While wandering around in complete anonymity could feel lonely and isolating, I found it could also be exhilarating. I went in and out of stores filled with beautiful clothing and shoes and finally headed toward the bus stop where I had been let out that morning.

Confirming the bus number and timetable, I thought the bus I needed would be arriving in about ten minutes. I didn't notice a lot of other tourists, in comparison to Florence, and once I got on the bus, they all seemed to be locals.

The bus was packed with people of all ages heading home from work or school, and as we weaved in and out of traffic and looped around a section of town I hadn't seen before, I began to get nervous. I leaned forward to ask the lady in the seat ahead of mine if I was on the correct bus. Long before I understood her words, I could see by her animated face that I was not! Fortunately her daughter, who was of school age and had, therefore, taken some English, jumped in to help me.

She explained to me that I needed to get off the bus as soon as possible, as we were headed out of Verona to, essentially, the suburbs. She gave me general directions back into the center of town, and I thanked her profusely as I got off at the next stop. It was beginning to get dark, and I debated stopping at a bar to ask if they could call a taxi for me. But the neighborhood had deteriorated quickly, and nervously, I kept moving toward the city.

Finally, I recognized the Castelvecchio Bridge, which meant I was back where I had started before my scenic ride on the bus with my new friends. I remembered a taxi stand being around the corner, so I headed that way. Once I was in the taxi on my way to the hotel, I relaxed some. The driver was an older gentleman who seemed keen on the idea of us sharing an Italian/English lesson, and I hadn't the heart to tell him I was exhausted. So I asked him all about his family and tried to stay awake as he named all of his grandchildren.

I opted to stay in my room and raid the mini bar rather than venture out again. I really just wanted a hot bath (I settled for a shower), a glass of wine, and my book. Climbing in the clean sheets, I laughed a bit, out loud. It had been a day, as usual, that was full of surprises, elegant scenery, and some excitement. The key to this new life of mine was simply not to get settled on a plan. Go with the flow—it's all an adventure!

Tomorrow I would be fifty-nine years old. I had been divorced for a decade, in Italy for almost two years, and very much all alone. I was living a life I never dreamed possible, never dreamed at all; yet, it was all okay. I was becoming more comfortable with uncertainty, more confident in my own abilities, and less dependent than ever on anyone else's approval.

I will never know if that confidence came from my move to Italy or my nearing sixty years old, but I was pleased it had arrived.

Forty-seven

Florence sweltered in the summer heat! Finally the ever-classy Florentine women dressed in loose-fitting dresses and comfortable sandals. Conversations with Italians centered around where one was going for *Ferragosto*.

This was my first August in Florence, and I didn't know about *Ferragosto*, the holiday that officially begins on August 15. Because all holidays in Italy have their roots in religion, it coincides with the Catholic feast of the Assumption of Mary. It is the last two weeks of August, when most of the city closes down and all the Florentines head to the beach.

Italians, not being confined to set rules, begin *Ferragosto* any time after the first of August, and it wasn't unusual for them to take the entire month off. This I learned by chatting with my friend Marco, who had a small *panino* shop by the Sant'Ambrogio market. I'd been drawn into his place by a sign that said he made a falafel panini, and I occasionally needed a break from the typical Italian *salume*.

Marco would often tell me of how dire times were in his business and how difficult it was to pay taxes and keep afloat in Italy. As he made my order, which he knew by now, he told me he would be shutting down in August.

"All of August?" I asked him, thinking that was a long vacation, and worried about where I might find my falafel fix.

"*Certo,*" he answered, meaning *of course!*

The American in me couldn't resist explaining to Marco that if *he* stayed open when all the other *panino* shops closed, he'd get all the business in town and make a killing!

Marco's face was classic Italian with the mixture of confusion and annoyance I had come to recognize. Complete with the hand gesture of scrambling an egg in one's palm, finger tips touching, he ranted on and on.

"But it's *Ferragosto*," he told me, as though he were speaking to someone intellectually impaired.

And after a few more rounds of us each explaining our point of view, ultimately Marco won. It's *Ferragosto*, and that tells you a lot of what motivates Italians. It's not all about making money, but rather tradition, culture, relationships. It's a concept our American brains struggle with but Italians won't budge from. It's how it's always been done.

I thought about the empty beaches that Pat and I had seen when we were in Monte Argentario; miles and miles of chairs and umbrellas sitting in the sun, just waiting for August to arrive. Once August did arrive, not a square inch of sand was to be found on the beach, and not a shop would be open outside of the center of Florence.

I took my falafel sandwich back across the bridge to my apartment in San Niccolò, hiked up the four flights of stairs, and wondered what August would be like when Florence became a ghost town, and everyone but the tourists headed to the beach.

I'd planned to meet Alexandra, at the Odeon Bistro, which was outside of the exquisite Odeon theater. Built in 1462 alongside Palazzo Strozzi, it has large, cushy chairs and old-school elegance. I loved going to movies there where I could read subtitles in Italian or English.

The Odeon Bistro, like almost all restaurants in Florence, sported linen tablecloths and napkins and, in the summer months, misters strained to cool the thick, hot air. I had just made the mistake of stopping at Max Mara to try on a dress

I'd seen in the window. As I struggled to get it over my head and past my shoulders, I'd called out to ask a reed-thin saleswoman for a larger size. She informed me that was the largest size they carried, and I slinked out of the shop thinking I was undeserving of lunch.

Meeting Alexandra as I walked in, she looked directly at me and exclaimed, "You just radiate! You're so beautiful!"

As I told her of my Max Mara horror story, she laughed and told me those stores were not made for American girls like us. I forgot that Alex was closer to the age of my children than to me, and I loved the time we spent together, whether in museums or at lunch. She became my best gal pal, one I truly let my guard down with, and we would candidly share frustrations of living in Italy, Italians, Americans, and expats.

On that day, she asked me a series of questions that went deeper than we had gone before, which led me to tell her of Thomas and my ex-husband, and how I had no money coming in. It was a part of my story that I rarely shared with anyone, and when I looked up at her face, her eyes were filled with tears.

"I know," was all I could say, but the gratitude I felt wash over me was huge. I had shared my deepest wound, and it had been met with compassion. Alexandra composed herself and called our server over. "We'll need two glasses of prosecco, please," she told him in flawless Italian. When they arrived, she toasted to me and my future, which she promised would be bright.

Forty-Eight

The breeze at dawn has secrets to tell you.
Don't go back to sleep; don't go back to sleep.
—Rumi

I heard Dr. Wayne Dyer speak many times, and he frequently quoted Rumi. Wayne has been my greatest teacher and mentor, and he would explain that in the darkness and stillness of the early morning, our thoughts are the most clear and connected to our soul. There were messages to receive, Dr. Dyer would say, and he would get up to do his best writing in those early-morning hours.

I'd wake up at about three a.m. all right, but I would awake in the hot summer stillness that July in a full panic. It seemed to be the hour my demons got up to play, and I would be lost in the sensation of drowning, alone and forgotten. Finally giving up on sleep, I'd untangle myself from the knotted sheets and walk out to the living room to look out at the shimmering palm trees lit by the moon.

The only secret the early dawn seemed to tell me was that I was alone and broke. My heart would race as I paced the length of my living area. *What am I going to do?* was the singular thought that looped over and over. I couldn't see how the tours could provide a living unless I got the word out to a wider audience, and even living on a small scale was quickly diminishing my cash reserves. I wondered how I would ever afford a home again without enough money for a down payment.

It was only on these nights, when I let go of all my bravado, that I faced my greatest fears. Perhaps I would always be alone, and perhaps I needed to leave Italy and find a real job in the U.S. I met those demons head-on many an early morning that July, as I was utterly out of ideas and quick to concede that they had the best of me.

I had come to Italy to find joy, and I had done that. I'd stood on my own two feet and become my own best friend. While proud of those accomplishments, those skills didn't pay the bills.

I'd worked to design a tour for other women to share my love of Tuscany, and it had worked—one time. The April tour had been a success, but I couldn't see the rest of the story, how it was going to continue. I'd written to magazines, travel companies, and women's groups to try to drum up some business, but nothing seemed to be happening to fill a tour in October. *Huffington Post* continued to publish and feature what I wrote, but while that gave me great street cred, it didn't seem to produce tour registrations or an income.

I told the night sky (and my demons) that I was afraid, really afraid. Then I waited to start the coffee until four-thirty a.m., which for some reason seemed like morning, not night.

By the time dawn lit the same palm trees in the Bardini Garden with her early-morning light, I felt better. I'd come this far on a wing and a prayer, and I wasn't about to let go of my dream. What is it about the dark, and the middle of the night, that makes life's problems and challenges seem so overwhelming?

Forty-nine

In mid-July I received an email from Shelley Emling, editor of *Huffington Post*'s "Post+50" section. Shelley wrote that the *Huffington Post*, in conjunction with Rita Wilson and NBC's *The Today Show*, was looking to spotlight fifty people over fifty who had reinvented their lives in a positive way.

Her mass email encouraged us to nominate ourselves, someone else, or spread the word. Shelley explained that the fifty people chosen would have their pictures and stories highlighted in a special *Huffington Post* section, and one or two of the fifty would be featured on *The Today Show*.

The last part of that sentence didn't even register with me. As I read of fifty people being spotlighted by *Huffington Post*, all I could think of was *free advertising!* If I was named one of those fifty, I could talk about the tours for women to Tuscany and surely convince some of those readers to sign up for a tour.

Writing to Sarah, a few friends, as well as the ladies from the April tour wasn't easy for me. I have never been comfortable asking for the spotlight, and I hesitated now to ask them to put me there. An introvert at heart, I could more easily nominate myself than ask others to do it for me. But I asked, and then I waited.

One of my favorite things about Florence is that right in the middle of the crowded city, one can find a secluded and quiet spot, almost like the secret clubhouse Gayle and I would build each summer of our childhood. Locals know where to find these places, and Amblé is a perfect example.

Not a block from the Arno River, just off of Ponte Vecchio, hidden behind an ivy-laced wall, is this delightful hideaway. The food is fresh, service friendly, and the freshly squeezed lemonade is a signature drink. As I sat down on the funky, school-style chairs on July 17, 2014, I pulled out my phone to check emails.

Immediately my eye was drawn to the one whose subject line was *TODAY SHOW, 50 OVER 50!*

I opened up the email as I waited for my sandwich to arrive.

It was from a woman who introduced herself as a producer with NBC's *The Today Show*. She explained that she'd received a submission from the *Huffington Post*'s "50 Over 50" project that they were working on together. Needless to say, she had my full attention!

The rest of the email asked how and where they could reach me to discuss my move to Florence and the new business. She concluded by asking if I would be interested in participating in a remote segment from Italy for their show.

My head was swimming as I reread the letter.

It didn't specifically say I'd been named one of *Huffington Post*'s fifty, but would I be interested in participating in a segment? I'd have to have been named one of the fifty if *The Today Show* contacted me, wouldn't I?

I thought about jumping up to ask my server if I could have my lunch to go, but I decided against it. There have been a few moments in my life when I had known something pivotal was occurring, and this was one of them. I wanted to sit in the shelter of the shade next to the ivy wall and look up at the tall buildings surrounding me, with their shuttered windows and centuries-old architecture. I wanted to memorize the moment and drink in the magic. Something really amazing had happened, *was* happening, and I wanted to be fully present in it.

I fired off an email with my Skype address as soon as I arrived back in my apartment, beginning my correspondence with the producers of the show. They'd continue to ask me for old pictures of me teaching fitness class, or my children when they were young, and I'd continue to explain that the reason I was to be featured was because I had left all of that behind in the United States...*where I no longer lived!* I was now living out of two suitcases, neither of which included old photo albums!

I had a local photographer shoot some photos and video in and around San Niccolò, Ponte alle Grazie, and up to my favorite church, San Miniato. Aldo Bustos was the photographer, and he seemed to have endless energy! He sprinted from one shot to another to get a new angle, and even though I could see the perspiration rolling down his face, he didn't want to quit until he was positive I had just what I needed.

The end of July in Florence, Italy, is not a time to hang outside for hours and be photographed! I felt like I was melting, certain any makeup I'd started the day wearing was long gone. I prayed that Aldo's camera would be kind.

By now I had determined I was to be named one of *Huffington Post*'s "50 Over 50," even if they hadn't notified me of such. The announcement was to be made on Monday, August 4, 2014, and that was the date *The Today Show* had given me as well for my story to run. Of course, they had qualified that with saying that should a big news story occur, I'd be bumped. Otherwise, I would be the kickoff person on the Kathie Lee and Hoda hour for the *Huffington Post* announcement.

I told close friends, of course, and warned my children that pictures of them were included in this very public event. I hesitated to announce it broadly for fear it wouldn't actually happen! But as the day grew closer, and the enormous amount of communication continued between the producer in New York City and me, I was thinking, short of another 9/11, that my story would be aired.

I sent an email to my hometown newspaper, *The Salt Lake Tribune*, and asked if they would be interested in a "local girl makes *The Today Show*" story. I heard back from one of their reporters, Kristen Moulton. She said the paper would be interested but would want to run their story the day after the show aired.

Kristen and I had a Skype session, and she sent me an additional list of questions as well. Having done quite a few radio interviews since moving to Florence, most of the questions I had answered before. It was surreal to talk about the *Today Show* and *Huffington Post* event as though it were really going to happen. I couldn't imagine how the actual day would feel.

Fifty

Italy is six hours ahead of the U.S. East Coast, so I had all morning of August 4 to walk around Florence, go to the market, and feel like it was any other day. While I felt the ground was rumbling under my feet in preparation for something big, I had no idea what would happen. I took comfort in that no one in Florence would be tuning into *The Today Show*, so if it was a disaster, I could hide out here forever!

HuffPost Live contacted me to see if I would join them for a segment immediately after *The Today Show* aired, which would include Elle MacPherson and an actress who had also been named as one of the "50 Over 50." I ran a sound and picture check with the technician ahead of time and knew that any personal calls and responses to the show would have to wait until the *HuffPost Live* segment had ended.

Friends on Facebook began posting pictures of the promo spots showing me standing on Ponte alle Grazie, with the famous Ponte Vecchio behind me and the *Today Show* logo and banner. "Reinvention after 50," it headlined, "One Woman's Life-Changing European Trip!"

Gulp.

The upcoming segment continued to be promoted with photos of me drinking coffee, and Kathie Lee and Hoda seated in front of a large panorama of Florence highlighted with the Duomo.

Gulp.

Seated alone at my dining room table, on the top floor of an ancient *palazzo* (which lacked air-conditioning), I had closed the windows and shutters to keep out the oppressive heat. I had a fan going, which I knew I would need to shut off once the live interview started, and a washcloth to dab the perspiration from my face.

Through the magic of Skype, at three fifty-three p.m. my time, I was able to watch the segment live, as Kathie Lee began with an introduction of *The Today Show*'s collaboration with *Huffington Post*'s "50 Over 50."

When I heard her say, "Lisa Condie was chosen from over a thousand submissions to *Huffington Post,*" I knew we were rolling!

"When Lisa was fifty-six, she took a trip to Italy with her daughter and had one of those *aha* moments…" and the rest, for me, was a blur.

I had done the voiceover for the video segment they played, which had photos and pictures from the spring tour and of my beloved Florence. As the segment ended, Hoda exclaimed, "I love her!" I took a deep breath and long exhale…it was over, and it had really happened!

I had placed my phone in the bedroom but left it on. I didn't have time between *The Today Show* airing and *HuffPost Live's* interview with Caroline Modarressy-Tehrani to check it. The interview lasted almost a half hour, and while it mostly focused on supermodel Elle, several times Caroline asked me a specific question, and I could see myself in a somewhat parallel universe answering on the screen!

At last it was all over, and I walked back to the bedroom to get my phone and stopped in the kitchen to pour myself a glass of wine. Before I sat back down at the computer to see the reaction, I walked to the window and looked out at the familiar outline of trees in the neighboring Bardini Garden.

Everything had gone perfectly. I was so grateful. No one had buzzed loudly at the door, and all had remained quiet in the courtyard below me. The miracle that was Wi-Fi had remained connected and working, and no large news event had bumped me until tomorrow.

"Thank you," I whispered to my angels, who I am certain played a part in orchestrating today. *Grazie mille*, I said as well, just in case a few of them were Italian.

I really only wanted to hear from my children, Shauna, and the Dodo girls. *Did you see it? Was I okay?*

I sent them a message that I was free and that they could call me on Skype, then clicked on to Facebook. My page had blown up! I had more notifications and friend requests than I could get through, and my news page was covered with friends posting about my morning. It was unbelievable!

After the rounds of calls from loved ones, I clicked on to my email. It had blown up as well!

I knew myself and my energy level, and so I called upon Scarlett O'Hara's advice once again and decided to think about all of that tomorrow. I was hungry for dinner but not company, so I walked down to BevoVino and found a quiet table in the back, away from the noise of the street.

Vincenzo greeted me, as usual, with a glass of prosecco and asked me what I wanted to eat. It was a relief that not even Vincenzo knew I'd had such a momentous day. Even if I had been able to explain it, *The Today Show* would mean nothing to them, and an interview with *HuffPost Live* would mean even less. I sat in the comfortable familiarity of this tiny *trattoria*, sipped my prosecco, and smiled. I knew I'd had a big day, and it had unfolded perfectly!

Fifty-one

The morning after *The Today Show* segment aired, I was eager to see if the *Salt Lake Tribune* had run my story. I went to the online version, which I read frequently while in Italy, and looked.

There was the article, complete with several photos, on the front page of the local section. As I read through the lengthy article, I was touched with the job that Kristen Moulten had done in writing my story. She captured, more than anyone else had, the essence of why I went to Italy and what I was hoping to do with the tour company.

The article noted that both Sarah and I were originally from Utah, and this business was something neither of us had done before. She mentioned that the trip I went on with my daughter was supposed to be with my "beau," which made me laugh—that was a term I hadn't heard in years!

I wondered what the reaction would be in the city I was raised in, and where I had spent most of my life. I hoped a couple of ex-beaus (as in an ex-husband and Thomas) had choked just a bit on their morning coffee! The girl I was when either of them knew me was long gone, with a much stronger version in her place. Their joint effort to punish me for leaving them had sent me reeling for a while, scared me, and shaken me to my core—but no longer.

———

Since *The Today Show* aired, every one of the tours has had someone in it who said that show was the moment they decided to come to Tuscany with me. I had no idea how many people watched morning television!

I had women tell me that the day my segment aired had been their only sick day in years, and as they watched the show they made their decision. The credibility I gained from both the segment on *The Today Show* and continually being featured by *Huffington Post* is something I will forever be grateful for. It was advertising I could not have purchased, and the incredible variety of people who it allowed me to meet has been life changing.

That said, I had no idea what was to come in the form of emails! Every morning for the next two weeks, I'd open my email to find pages and pages of letters. Mostly, I had become the *Dear Abby of Lonely Hearts Over Fifty*—generally women whose husbands had left them, and they wanted to come to Italy.

Many letters would get right to the point and ask if I could help get them a visa! Those were the easy ones to answer—sorry, no.

Requests for interviews poured in, and even a few for Italian publications. Emails from childhood friends whom I hadn't seen in forty years filled my inbox, and I received hundreds of friend requests on Facebook.

For me, it was a mixture of emotion—I'd never wanted the spotlight and had grown comfortable with my anonymity in Italy. I prayed the publicity would translate into actual bodies signing up for the tours, and it confirmed to me that many women over fifty were looking for their joy. It was rewarding to think I could help them in some small way, through writing, speaking, and the tours of Tuscany.

The metaphor of going with the current seemed appropriate here, as the best things in my life had just organically appeared. I reminded myself that whether they appeared in the form of a relationship or even a career, if I tried to push the boulder upstream, it never worked. Riding the current of life's flow, trusting in the energy of the Universe in directing me always provided the best results and the greatest peace.

And so it was now, as my new career and life in Italy seemed to gel, I was getting the message. I could share my story with others and encourage them to find their own passion and joy. I was being asked not to shrink from the spotlight and push others to shine, as I had so often, but to take the spotlight and encourage others to do the same. The best version of oneself is not in living small; that, I knew now, only brought regrets.

To commemorate this glorious gift I'd been given, I ordered a bracelet from my friend, Laura Wandry. She is a remarkable silversmith who spends part of her time in Florence. I sketched out the familiar words, "Woman of Courage," and had them separated by the *fleur-de-lis*–shaped "Gillies of Florence," and she designed the rest. We collaborated each step of the way as she cut, by hand, the intricate designs and each letter. It is elegant and feminine, a constant reminder to me of the courage I had to jump off the cliff, confident that my wings would sprout before I hit the ground.

Fifty-two

Despite all the fabulous events of August, I had one lingering problem that I knew I had to get working on. My *Permesso di soggiorno* had to be renewed. If my two years in Italy had taught me nothing else, they taught me that anything involving the bureaucracy of Italy would not be a smooth, quick, nor pleasurable experience.

It was a renewal, however, so it's not like this was my first rodeo. And any time I hear the word "renewal" I tend to think the process is going to be easier. It's why I never let my Utah driver's license expire. I always want the renewal option and never the start-all-over option. As I began the process to renew my *permesso*, I didn't dream it would be as daunting as the first time.

Add that to the list of lessons learned in Italy.

One question that I am asked, almost as often as how I live legally in Italy, is why I don't write a how-to book on the process. Think of all the Americans yearning to be expats who would buy it, and all the wisdom I could pass on! (Think of all the money I could make!) This chapter is dedicated to answering that comment.

I began gathering all the necessary documents and letters for my *permesso* renewal about sixty days before my initial one was to expire. While I was standing in line at the post office to buy the kit, I thought how the process would be much easier now. I knew which *sportello* I was to go to, and I knew how to obtain a number from the machine outside.

I had also been in Italy long enough by now to know that as soon as I was at the front of the line, some huffing, puffing, old Italian, who just needed to ask *one* question, would swoop in from the side and ask me if they could go next. I'd been around this block before, and I answered "NO!"

With the aid of my Italian friend, we (okay, she) filled out the forms. There is no wiggle room here if you make a mistake—for instance, using blue ink instead of black. I confidently had her check the two-year box option, thinking an extra year of a *permesso* for twenty euro was a bargain.

Copies and documents, pictures and letters, and about a month's worth of work later, I sent the packet in. In return, I received the date to pick up my new *permesso* at the Questura.

The Questura. There are just no words to really describe what it's like to spend a few hours (it will never be less than that) at the Questura in Florence, Italy. Suffice it to say, you will want to take a shower afterward.

I arrived early at the Questura, as I always did. The time frame given in the paperwork means nothing. The number you hold means everything. An early-morning walk had me there well before my allotted time, but the officer gave me a number anyway, and I took my seat on the dreadfully uncomfortable benches provided.

Once my number was flashed on the overhead screen, I jumped up like I had won the lottery. The woman at the window was pleasant enough as she led me through the fingerprinting ritual and perused my documents. Everything at the Questura is done in Italian, and there's no slowing down for the newbies.

After a few minutes, she handed me a piece of paper that said I could come back to pick up my *permesso* after I had obtained a certificate of residency.

Arrivederci.

I wasn't surprised. I knew from the other expats that I was probably going to be required to obtain the certificate before they would renew my *permesso*. Yes, some get by without, but apparently, I wasn't going to be one of them.

Sounds simple enough, right? Just one more document and I was good to go!

One must apply for the certificate of residency, which means one must first find the proper form. Since this is Italy, the form couldn't be downloaded from a website or conveniently picked up at any post office. It took two American expats (both of us pretty smart gals), two days, one bus ride, two offices, miles of walking and multiple telephone calls just to *obtain* the form.

Once I arrived at the correct office, retrieved my number, and waited my turn, I took my seat across from the agency representative. She asked what I needed, and I explained I was here for the form that was required for the certificate of residency. As I did so, my eyes dropped to the stack of forms on her desk, and I could clearly see they were the forms I needed.

Curtly, the woman told me that I needed an appointment to come in and get the form, that I couldn't just arrive and take a number.

Having been here a while, I just said, "No, I called yesterday, and I am here now," and, pointing to the form on her desk, continued, "and that's the form I need."

I've learned a thing or two about being pushy during my time here.

After calling in a supervisor, which included the required ten minutes of bickering back and forth, she relented and handed me the form.

Arrivederci.

Another onslaught of paperwork, including a copy of my new apartment contract, and the paperwork was ready to be submitted to Palazzo Vecchio, the town hall of Florence. The historic palazzo was just minutes from my place on via di Mezzo, and a walk I always enjoyed, but upon arriving at the governmental office, I was told the package had to be mailed, not dropped off. And so, mail it I did.

I received a call a few days later from a nice gentleman at the palazzo who informed me that my paperwork had arrived, but the apartment contract had not been properly registered. I told him not to worry (pretty sure he wasn't), that I would contact my landlord and check into it. I contacted Lorenzo, he checked into why the registration hadn't been noted, and we eventually were able to get a copy for me.

I resubmitted the entire packet, with the new apartment registration, at my local post office. I had just done this a few weeks before, so I was confident in the process of asking to send the packet to Palazzo Vecchio by registered mail.

The woman helping me at the post office kept asking for my phone number in London. Of course, this conversation was in such rapid Italian, I thought I was misunderstanding what she was saying. I continued to look puzzled at her asking me about *Londra.*

She ramped it up a few notches, which happens quickly here, until everyone around us was watching the drama. Finally, I took a stab at answering her and explained, in Italian, that I didn't live in London; I was from the United States, but I now lived in Florence. In full exasperation, she threw her hands in the air and sighed loudly. Just as quickly as it had begun, it was over. The packet was taken.

Arrivederci.

A few days later, I received a call from Palazzo Vecchio. (I recognized the number this time!) On the other end of the line was a woman who informed me that I needed to come to the palazzo this very afternoon.

She proceeded to ask me, item by item, for every bit of information I sent in. Before I would reply, I could hear the shuffling of papers, and she would say, "Never mind, I have it."

Finally she informed me it was all just fine, don't bother coming to the palazzo. She also informed me that someone from the city would be by to verify that I was living at the address I had provided, and that could occur anytime within the next six weeks. I wondered if I was supposed to sit home for six weeks and wait.

However, the very next day a gentleman buzzed at the front door and identified himself as the investigator who was to establish that I was Lisa Condie and did, in fact, reside at this address. It took five minutes and was the easiest part of the whole process.

A few days after the visit, the self-addressed envelope arrived from Palazzo Vecchio containing the *anagrafe*, the official registration, I needed to obtain my certificate of residency for my *permesso*.

On a humid morning mid September, I walked to the *parterre* with the *anagrafe* to obtain my certificate of residency. The *parterre* is a small government office, and much newer than the Questura. It had fairly comfortable chairs and was not nearly as dreary an atmosphere as hangs in the other government buildings of Florence.

I obtained my number by the front door and sat down in the waiting area, eager to people-watch. A lovely blonde woman about my age immediately sat down next to me and struck up conversation. For thirty-five years, she had split her time between Switzerland and Italy. Since she was Swiss, I figured she would have an idea or two on organizing this dog-and-pony show, and all it took was for me to ask one question! Much to my amusement, she gave me an onslaught of opinions on how disorganized this system was, and I was almost sorry when my number appeared on the screen overhead.

My number directed me to booth number seven, where I was seated across from a woman who obviously hated her job. She asked what I was there to do, and I explained my mission, that I needed a card of residency. I immediately opened the *anagrafe* and slid it over to her side of the desk.

The clerk pretended for a few minutes to not have any idea what I was talking about, and I repeated the request an additional three times. It wasn't until the third time through that I realized I had said *carte* (card) not *certificarto* (certificate). Once we cleared up that huge misunderstanding, she sighed, typed out the certificate, and asked for €16.52.

I dug deep into my wallet and produced fifty-two cents, which I added to a twenty-euro bill, and proudly handed them over. (How many people come up with the exact fifty-two cents?)

Didn't I have one euro? she wanted to know. I rummaged through the coin pocket of my wallet. No, I didn't. She glared. Intimidated by the glare, I rummaged through my wallet again, in case one had hatched in the last thirty seconds. "No," I assured her again, I didn't have another euro.

Exasperated, she was forced to hand me four single euros and said I could go. Not *arrivederci*—just "Go." In English.

I don't know what it is about Italians and exact change, but they will wait forever for you to locate it, and thank you profusely if you do.

I had to take the newly acquired certificate of residency to *sportello H* at the Questura, and numbers for that window are only given out between seven a.m. and nine a.m. I arrived around eight fifteen a.m. the following morning. The main lobby was packed, and I was handed a piece of paper with my number—754. Ouch.

I watched the numbers tick off long enough to establish I had at least an hour before mine would be close and left to walk across the park to a bar for a coffee. Trust me, one would rather be anywhere than the Questura.

Upon returning, I was pleasantly surprised to see that better progress than I anticipated had taken place, and I was probably just twenty minutes away. I was picturing that I would whip out that certificate and they would hand over my *permesso*, and all would be right in the world, or at least my world.

The man behind the *sportello* window smiled as he said hello to me. Let me say that again. He smiled. At me. I was thinking he wouldn't last long at the Questura.

We were having a pleasant conversation in Italian when he introduced the word *problema* into the sentence. I picked up most of the meaning: because I had moved, there was a problem, and the information wasn't all the same.

I assured him, no problem. (Oh, please, not a problem at this late date.) The certificate of residency has my current address on it, I assured him. Check it. No problem.

Once he rechecked it, we had a good laugh. No problem! We talked about San Niccolò versus Borgo Pinti, my new neighborhood, but I still had sweat dripping down my back over the word *problema*. He verified my phone number and got up from his chair. My new *permesso* was so close, I could almost feel it in my hand!

The gentleman returned with a sheet of paper, handed it to me, and said within a month, I would receive a text on my phone, notifying me that my *permesso* was ready to be picked up. Sigh.

So close. But obviously, this time, it was really just one more step away.

As soon as I left the Questura, I realized he had taken my new certificate of residency, and I had failed to make a copy of it. That was such a rookie mistake. How was it that I had forgotten the cardinal rule of *permesso* work? Make copies of *everything*.

A couple of weeks later, a text arrived on my phone indicating my new *permesso* was ready for pick up. When I finally held it in my hand, the first thing I looked at was the expiration date. September 12, 2016—two years away!

Year Three ~ 2014

Prologue

But little by little,
as you left their voices behind,
the stars began to burn
through the sheets of clouds,
and there was a new voice,
which you slowly
recognized as your own,
that kept you company
as you strode deeper and deeper
into the world,
determined to do
the only thing you could do—
determined to save
the only life you could save.
—excerpt from *The Journey* by Mary Oliver

My third year in Italy began with the sense that this was home—comfortable and familiar. Like lovers who had stayed around long enough to see past infatuation, we both had our faults, but we'd learned to amicably work through our differences.

I will always rail against the sea of red tape that is Italy's bureaucracy, but I had successfully navigated obtaining permission for another two years of living here legally—no small feat. I could sigh in exasperation over yet another strike of some sort, or the grossly inefficient way the grocery stores were designed, but ultimately, I had adapted.

The elegance of dressing, even for everyday errands, now seemed second nature to me. I was living small, and that had taught me to invest in quality pieces of clothing, shoes, and purses when I did spend. It seemed only right to dress in classic clothing while walking by the Palazzo Vecchio with the gorgeous open loggia of original statues and other Florentine treasures.

Rarely did I go out that I didn't bump into someone I knew on the street or in the markets. Particularly now that the busiest tourist months were over, I would stop in to say hello to Francesca at *Principessa Cristalli d'Autore* or wander through *AquaFlor* and visit with Caitlin. It felt good to be connected to the city, and afternoon store closings, as well as *aperitivo* time, matched the rhythm of my daily life.

Italy, for its part, seemed to accept me as well. My Italian was not beautiful, but most were forgiving and gracious when I conversed in their language. I would laugh, rather than be insulted, if they switched to English at hearing my accent, and I continued to find Italians extraordinarily generous.

On occasion, particularly in business dealings, I would become "too American" and jump right into discussing money, or be too aggressive in trying to hurry an interaction along. The subtle clues, and the not so subtle—such as switching to formal salutations instead of friendly ones—would let me know I'd overstepped my reach. I made many apologies, some for my guests and some for me, and was always graciously forgiven.

Love has a way of showing—on one's face, the eyes, the voice, and general manner. I think that's what Italians saw in me. They sensed I loved them, their country, and their culture. I didn't want to just drop in for a month and indulge in all their treasures, only to leave again. I was there to stay. I'd put in my time and now was accepted—flaws and all.

Fifty-three

Brenè Brown defines vulnerability as uncertainty, risk, and emotional exposure.

I was feeling some of that as emails continued to pour in, as well as the unsettling realization that strangers thought they knew me or at least knew my story.

As I read my email in the morning, many letters would begin, "I am just like you…" or "You are living my story, my dream…" It was a stark contrast to the rest of my day, walking around my new neighborhood of Borgo Pinti where few people knew my story.

As a result, I changed my morning routine. It used to begin with a brief stop in the kitchen for a cup of coffee and then straight to my computer to read emails.

I found that was a bit too much now, and though the stop at the kitchen for a cup of coffee was still the first thing I did, the second was to sit down and quietly welcome the day.

Sometimes that involved a meditation, but often I would light a candle, open the side doors to the courtyard and just look at the new day arriving. I felt a sense of responsibility to answer many of the emails and give them a thoughtful response. They would often be filled with someone's heartache or desire, and I wanted to answer with compassion.

A lot of emails were business related—either about the tours, if I needed a new assistant, or to schedule an interview.

I wanted to approach those with the appropriate amount of thought and respect as well.

So, I carved out some quiet time in the morning now, before the onslaught of the day began, to get centered.

I liked my new apartment in the Borgo Pinti neighborhood. It comprised mostly Italians but also had an international feel to it with lots of artisans and small *trattorias*. Under L'Arco di San Pierino were several *panino* shops and bars, with Pasticceria Patrizio Cosi, Borgo alle Fate, Ristorante Natalino, and the gorgeous (but expensive) fruit stand in Piazza Albizzi. I realized by now, I rarely needed to or cared to cook at home.

I didn't notice until I'd been in the apartment for a month that it didn't have an oven! Cooking was restricted to just a couple of burners on the stove and an inconveniently placed microwave beneath them, with a Barbie-sized refrigerator to the side. It was all I needed, and I found washing the few dishes I did use by hand rather relaxing.

My new washing machine had a built-in dryer, which originally sounded like a great idea! However, the temperamental machine would underdry as often as it would render my clothing six sizes too small, so I only used it for socks and towels. My clothes were strewn all over the apartment to dry, just as they had been in San Niccolò.

I had spent so much time alone in the past couple of years, that it was comfortable to me now. I liked being in earshot of a multitude of languages and ethnicities. While during the first year I had walked through the city not knowing anyone, as my third year in Florence was beginning, there was a familiar set of faces in my daily routine, and I had a sense of being connected to the city.

Alexandra would call most every morning on her bus ride into the city, to see what my plans were and to catch me up on hers. Often she would need to do a practice run of a museum or church for an upcoming tour, and I would gladly tag along as her guinea pig. I am certain, to this day, Alexandra had no idea how little I knew of Dante and Renaissance art. She opened up an exquisite world to me, which I eagerly entered, and she generously shared her knowledge on subjects I had known little or nothing about.

Andrea and Donatella were like my Italian relatives, checking in on me and making certain we had a weekly lunch or dinner together. Donatella would scold me if I hadn't phoned for a day or two or if, God forbid, I had gone to the doctor without her! In Italy, apparently, no woman goes to the doctor alone, and although a few years younger than me, Donatella seemed like my auntie.

After *The Today Show* aired, the expat and English-speaking community reached out to me from all over Florence and Italy. It was fun to get to know the faces behind famous blogs or publications. *The Florentine*, a new English magazine all expats read, invited me to many of their events.

Opening nights at Palazzo Strozzi, benefits at Palazzo Tornabuoni, and even a private tour with author Dr. Victor Coonin to visit Michelangelo's *David* kept my calendar busier than it had been in the previous two years. The timing was perfect, as I was hitting my stride with the business and confidence in my new life.

I had been named one of the "Tuscany Faces" and was interviewed by Georgette Jupe for *Italy Magazine*. She and *Lost in Florence*'s Nardia Plumridge became great gal pals on the social scene. I was older than most of the social networkers in Florence, but they welcomed me with open arms as we found ourselves at many of the same events together. Georgette, Nardia, Alexandra, and I would meet frequently for a coffee or lunch at the Gucci Caffé, and it felt good to have a tight network of women friends around me.

I decided to embrace the vulnerability of this new phenomenon—being known—although it was quite a departure from the privacy I had before. When people met me, they often already knew my story. It pushed me to find a new type of courage, and I embraced being transparent, utterly honest, and open. Again, I will never know if that transparency would have evolved with age or if it was a result of my journey to Italy. My thoughts, my words, and my actions were coming into alignment, and I felt comfortable in my skin, my new neighborhood, and life in Italy.

Fifty-four

Every morning around eight-thirty, an older gentleman unlocked the enormous double doors that led into the courtyard of my apartment building from via di Mezzo. Large enough for many cars to be parked, this area was where my long windows opened to, and the sounds from the other apartments and the neighborhood would fill mine, reminding me I wasn't alone.

The palazzo on via di Mezzo was six hundred years old. My door was under a bust of Dante, and across the hall was a similar bust of Michelangelo. The walls of the palazzo were so thick that it was tomb-like with the windows closed, and I couldn't get Wi-Fi or cell service in any room of my apartment but the main one.

Daily, this gentleman drove his car into the very large area and parked outside a workspace that opened up to the community courtyard. Puttering around the car, he'd whistle eight notes of a melody in an endless loop as he'd close the main doors again and head to his workshop. Needless to say, I became familiar with the eight-note tune.

I called him, in my mind, Mister Rogers, because he wore a light button-down cardigan sweater every day, regardless of the weather. He had a thick head of white hair, and while he moved a little slowly, he was nimble and agile as he unloaded equipment from his car to his work area.

Lorenzo had arranged for a new hot water heater to be installed in my bathroom. I'd had enough freezing cold showers and was looking forward to its arrival. Right on schedule, a man pulled a large white van into the courtyard, buzzed at my door, and went to work installing the new water heater. Twenty minutes later, he hauled the old one out and loaded it in his truck.

Two minutes later, my doorbell rang. Thinking the repairman had forgotten something, I flung the door wide open and found myself face to face with Mister Rogers. He immediately began yelling at me, his face becoming redder with each minute and accusation.

It was rapid-fire Italian, but I picked up that he was furious the repairman had parked in the (his) courtyard. Mister Rogers wanted to know why I had let him in the main doors and allowed him to park. I told him I hadn't and that Lorenzo must have given him a key, and with that he exploded, calling me a liar and a few other names—I'm guessing.

The real Mister Rogers would never have behaved so poorly.

The repairman apparently heard the yelling and got out of his truck to come defend either me or himself; I couldn't tell which. That escalated into a shouting match between the two of them, and I was just about to close my door to it all, when an upstairs neighbor arrived and joined the commotion. I'm not certain whose side he was on, but I put my hands up (typical Italian gesture) and walked back into my apartment.

A few minutes later, I saw the white truck pull out of the courtyard.

A few minutes after that, my doorbell buzzed again.

Opening it more cautiously this time, I was, once more, face to face with Mister Rogers.

He lit into the same dialogue, reminding me I didn't have permission to let someone in through the main doors or park in the courtyard, and while he stood under Dante and continued his tirade, I calmly closed the door.

As I sat on my couch in my stone-silent apartment, I felt a little shaken. Tears started to pool in my eyes, and I felt terribly alone. That lasted for about two and a half minutes.

Something started to rise up in me, seemingly from the ground below, until it filled my lungs, and I exhaled, "Oh, hell no!"

I wasn't going to take his anger or his berating me. The days of being someone's punching bag, either physically or verbally, were over. I didn't need to return his anger with my own, nor did I desire to be rude to the misnamed Mister Rogers, but I wouldn't acknowledge him either.

It has served people in my life for me to play small, and one of the truths I had uncovered about myself in the past few years was that *I wouldn't do that anymore*. While not confrontational, I'm no longer a people pleaser at any cost. That's the gift of self-love and self-respect; once you have it, others don't get to discharge their unhappiness and leave it at your doorstep.

Mister Rogers and I were mutually chilly to one another for a month or so as we passed in the doorway or on our street. I didn't go out of my way to avoid him—I certainly wasn't rude to him, but I simply ignored him.

And then, one late afternoon in October, when dusk seems to fall on Florence around four-thirty in the afternoon, Mister Rogers stood outside the large palazzo doors as I was leaving. He looked right at me, and I met his gaze.

"*Buona sera, Signora,*" he said, respectfully.

"*Buona sera,*" I replied.

Détente.

Fifty-five

Florence is a magnet to those who love to travel, and I found a steady stream of people who would visit. Justin's job would bring him to Europe a couple of times a year, and he would stay with me for a week or so, filling my days and my apartment with a familiar sense of family.

I love the fall, and it doesn't start to arrive in Florence until October. On a perfect autumn day, Justin and I traveled with Andrea and Donatella through the Chianti region, allowing Andrea to teach us about this area he knew so well. We visited small, family-owned wineries and *trattorias* and saw the picturesque countryside of Tuscany. The leaves were just beginning to change as we wove our way through the back roads and small towns, accessible only by car, and visited people and restaurants that they knew well.

I loved having Justin visit! Not just for the obvious reason that I adore my son, but since he'd been to Florence several times and seen the main attractions, we'd travel outside the city or go to lesser-known venues. He acclimated quickly to my new neighborhood, the local market, and the bars where he became a local for a few weeks.

Late one evening in October, Lorenzo called and explained he had a situation with a couple from the United States and could I help him. I said of course, and we agreed to meet the next morning at eight-thirty. As usual, I had no idea what

Lorenzo needed or wanted, but by now I trusted him—and he had never disappointed me!

I arrived outside of one of Lorenzo's many apartments in central Florence, and Lorenzo kissed my cheeks with the customary greeting and thanked me profusely for coming. He explained, as best he could in English and Italian, that an American couple had arrived in the night, and somewhere in their travels, they had lost a purse.

As he didn't speak a lot of English, Lorenzo couldn't communicate properly how to help them, and that's where I would come in.

Entering one of Lorenzo's more beautiful apartments, with a full terrace overlooking via dei Tosinghi (suffice it to say I'd never stayed there), I walked in on an obviously distressed couple.

I introduced myself and asked the woman, Kim, to tell me what had happened. Her husband looked up from the computer to nod hello, as he was trying to determine if charges had been made on their missing cards.

Kim was sleep-deprived and frustrated as she relayed their story. Due to an airline strike, they had opted to take the train from Paris to Florence. That had brought its share of mishaps and misery, and somewhere along in the train and taxi rides, a purse had been lost, stolen, or left.

As she continued with the details, tears began to roll down her cheeks, and I learned that the purse had contained both of their passports, all their credit cards, and nine-thousand euro.

With the last bit of information, I'm sure my face gave away what I was thinking. I couldn't imagine carrying that much cash in one place, and she slowly nodded before I said a word.

A friend at a bank had exchanged their dollars to euro without charging them a fee, and so they decided to get all the cash they thought they'd need for a month in Tuscany. They were to leave Florence after a week, travel some, and then meet their children and grandchildren at a villa in the Tuscan countryside.

What had sounded like a dream vacation had turned into a traveler's nightmare.

I looked up at Lorenzo who was obviously worried. He is the consummate host, and his goal is always to ensure his guests are happy and enjoying their time in Florence. That certainly wasn't the case right now.

I explained to Lorenzo, in Italian, what Kim had told me and also what I thought we needed to do. First stop would be the U.S. Embassy to acquire temporary passports.

Kim's husband, Dale, pushed away from the computer and came to give us an update. So far, no charges on the credit cards, but he knew they needed to be cancelled and new ones sent overnight to Lorenzo's address.

It was the middle of the night in the U.S., so a few calls had to wait. I chatted with Dale a minute, Lorenzo left to get some pastries for breakfast, and then I told them that we had to get them new passports. *Today*. Passports are a traveler's identification, and one can't go anywhere without them.

I called the U.S. Embassy to verify their hours and told Kim and Dale I would go with them to get new passports. They looked relieved, but still so sad.

Lorenzo returned with breakfast, but his new guests didn't feel up to eating. I told him we were going to the U.S. Embassy.

Walking in the fall sunshine, Dale and Kim told me about themselves, their combined family, and their love of Italy. I told them my story of arriving here as well, and how I'd wondered if Lorenzo really existed!

Once at the embassy we waited outside, watching the birds swoop down on the Arno and across to the ancient Oltrarno buildings. Finally, the guard indicated it was their turn, and I waited out in the sunshine for them.

The process at the embassy was quite simple, so Dale and Kim were surprised when I said our next stop, the Carabinieri to file an official report, would not be as pleasant.

While handsome in their Armani-designed uniforms, the officers of the police force, Carabinieri, are just not nice. I'd had to file a report when my credit card had been cloned my first year in Florence, and I remember how shocked I was that, in comparison to every other Italian I'd met, this division of the police force's officers were often flat-out rude.

It is well known in the expat community that a trip to the Carabinieri will not be an experience to treasure.

The show that ensued lived up to my warning, and I encouraged Kim and Dale to laugh at it rather than be offended. The officer took down the information begrudgingly, sneering at what was obviously contempt for either Americans or tourists in general. I did my best to answer his questions and shield Kim and Dale from his hostility. When I told him, in Italian, how much money had been lost, he shrugged his shoulders in indifference.

Once we left there, we did have a good laugh at the lack of the *bella figura* at the police station, and I could see their mood was lifted. When Dale asked where we could have lunch, I took it as a great sign that he was hungry.

Seated at La Bussola, still one of my favorite spots for great food and friendly Italian servers, we continued to share our stories. They were so kind and quick to decide that, while this start to their vacation had been disastrous, they didn't want the rest of the vacation to be. I was amazed at their resilience and attitude, and we toasted with *prosecco* to new friendships and brighter days ahead.

We exchanged contact information, and I dropped them off at their apartment for some much-needed rest.

One week later, I gathered with Lorenzo and his wife, Letizia, as well as Kim and Dale and their extended family for dinner. Relaxed and happy, they were joined by their children and grandchildren at a spacious villa outside of Florence. Views of rolling hills and olive trees stretched out in the Tuscan landscape, and Kim and I walked out on the patio together to see the sunset.

They'd had a wonderful time in Italy, despite the disastrous start, and with their children and grandchildren scattered through the villa, rest and relaxation restored Kim's spirit.

With the help of a chef, the family prepared a gorgeous spread of Italian courses for our dinner. I relished translating the conversations for Lorenzo and Letizia, as they usually had to do that at dinners for me!

Over the next several hours, we laughed, talked, and toasted to friendship! Despite never hearing a word about the lost purse, we were three generations with two languages and one story that had joyfully brought us all together.

Fifty-six

Besides the days in Chianti with Andrea and Donatella, Justin and I tried out a new tour with Walkabout Florence. The company was a favorite of mine, not just for the quality of their tours but also their outstanding customer service and guides. I'd done their Best of Tuscany and Cinque Terre tours many times, but the new Chianti Wine and Food Safari sounded intriguing! Justin and I were in heaven sampling wine and new olive oil for ten hours as well as climbing to the top of an ancient castle to view the panorama of the Chianti countryside.

I had just said goodbye to my son in October 2014 when I packed a small suitcase to fly to Barcelona and meet my dearest girlfriend, Sherrilee, and some of her family. They had finished a cruise and were extending their vacation time in one of my favorite cities, so I booked a cheap flight and headed an hour and forty-five minutes west to Spain.

After a few days of touring with the group through Barcelona, Sherrilee and I ventured out by ourselves for dinner on La Rambla, a tree-lined pedestrian mall in central Barcelona.

Barcelona's most famous street was bustling under the streetlamps outside the restaurant, and its view was a peek into Catalan culture. We'd walked it during the day, filled with pedestrians, souvenir hawkers, artists, mimes, and betting games for the gullible. It seemed just as alive at night, where dinnertime begins around nine, and the streets stay humming with a vibrant nightlife.

The food, sights, and sounds of Barcelona are so different than Florence, and as we situated our purses safely under the table to order dinner, I took out my newly purchased phone for a few photos. Couples walked arm in arm, groups of teenagers and tourists filled the wide street in the still-warm air of an autumn evening. I took a few pictures of my darling friend in her new fedora with the lights of La Rambla twinkling in the background.

A young man begging came by the table, and when I shook my head, he took out a sheet of paper with a baby's photo on it and asked again. Sherrilee and I both said a gentle *no*, and he was gone.

I perused the menu, which offered an array of wine and meat dishes so different than a *trattoria* of Florence. The heater lights overhead bathed us in gold, and we ordered wine and dinner and got back to the business of old friends catching up. Suddenly, a tall, well-built man rushed up to our table, sat down in the empty chair and flashed a police badge. He asked if either of us were missing a cell phone.

That was the first time I had noticed mine was no longer to the left of my fork! Shocked, I looked back at the officer as he pulled out my cell phone, recognizable with its bright pink cover, to hand back to me. While the encounter seemed odd and had caught me by surprise, the wheels in my mind started to turn. I'd been had by one of the oldest tricks in the book, and one that I'd warned my guests about! The young man begging at our table had covered my phone with the sheet of paper and then grabbed it!

But how had this man, who I now noticed was perspiring and panting a bit, come into having my phone? He explained that the police regularly patrol and watch for petty theft, which is so common on La Rambla. He'd seen the thief leave our table and start to run, so he chased him down, discovered my phone, and another police officer had taken the man to jail.

I was a little skeptical of the whole story. I couldn't believe I'd been lucky enough to have a police officer watching in the wings to catch my thief in action. I filled out some paperwork and none of the information seemed out of line, just basic identification and estimate of the phone's worth, time, and date sort of thing.

I looked at the officer again, a bit suspiciously this time, and he relayed the details once more until I finally relaxed. With a drop-dead gorgeous smile, this handsome policeman convinced me he was who he said he was. Sherrilee and I tried a couple of times to buy him dinner, but he refused.

As he left, our meals arrived, and we asked the server if she recognized the man who had been seated with us. She said she did and confirmed he worked for the police.

The next morning, I asked at the front desk of our hotel for directions to the closest police department. I'd been given copies of all the papers I'd filled out and signed, but I still wanted confirmation before I left Spain that they were legit.

While I walked across the park, the sun shone brightly on this October morning, and I descended to the basement of a large, white government building. The lady behind the glass thought my question a bit odd, but she did speak English and confirmed that the papers I had were official police copies.

My love for Catalonia's capital city grew even more that day as I hurried back to meet the group for a tour of Gaudi's Sagrada Familia! Barcelona is not only beautiful, but a strong, handsome policeman here could teach the Carabinieri in Florence a thing or two!

Fifty-seven

Ever since I first spotted the majestic church on the hill, I walked up to San Miniato Cemetery once a week. In November, the cemetery closes at dusk around four-thirty, but I wouldn't have wanted to linger there after dusk anyway.

While the church of San Miniato is a cool and quiet retreat after my hike up its steps, it's the enormous cemetery behind the church that I am drawn to. Acres and acres of mausoleums, headstones, and statues kept me endlessly interested in the history and stories of the Florentine families buried there.

Often among the headstones are pictures and poems of the once-alive Florentines. Elaborate statues and tributes to the deceased are there, many now covered with moss or black lichen or in various states of deterioration.

I wondered about reincarnation, as I weaved among the seemingly endless rows of graves, if I were there as well, after living a life as a Florentine centuries ago. I felt so connected to this city, to this place, and pondered the thought that if living one time was any less of a miracle than living multiple lifetimes. Were there ancient stories in my DNA that had drawn me to this country where I felt so at home? Was the rhythm of life in Tuscany forged in me centuries ago and had now been rediscovered in this new life?

I do know that there is an evolutionary path within a lifetime, and I have found it to be at the highest when I resist the least. Joy streamed into my daily life on those gentle November days when writing, reading, thinking, and walking occupied my hours. I realized with each passing month that I had achieved what I'd hoped to; I had become my own best friend, and I felt comfortable in my own skin.

The bells from the church tower always alarmed me when I was walking in the cemetery, but they gave me a heads-up to watch the time. I was utterly lost in my own world of thought when I was at San Miniato, so endlessly curious that the hours would pass unnoticed. The warning bells from the tower would alert me that it was time to head down the hill, across the bridge to my apartment. But first, I always stopped to say goodbye to the imposing angel statue that watches over the headstones by the exit.

I spent Thanksgiving with Donatella and Andrea in 2014 at a small restaurant near Sant'Ambrogio. It had become, for me, almost another regular day as it was, of course, for Italians. I'd had some shopping to do in the market, and Donatella joined me as Andrea ran some errands of his own. We talked of my upcoming trip to the United States, and Donatella expressed her worry that I wouldn't want to come back to Florence after being with my friends and family. I assured her I would, that I would only be away for three weeks, and reminded her that the little I did own would remain in my apartment!

Tours were filling for the spring months, and writing and promoting the business took many hours a day, so time out with my dearest friends was a treat. Even though I had a seven a.m. flight out of Florence, Donatella was adamant that Andrea take me to the airport. I assured her that I could arrange for a taxi to pick me up at five a.m., and then glanced at Andrea, who had a look of total relief on his face! I knew had I agreed with Donatella, he would have said yes, in a heartbeat, but his expression told me he was happy I hadn't!

I still had another week in Florence but knew Donatella and Andrea wouldn't be back into the city before I left, so we said goodbye, which involved many hugs and a few tears. Saying goodbye to an Italian, either on the phone or in person, is never a quick experience anyway, but this one definitely took a while. I'd walked about half a block when I turned around to see them both still standing outside the restaurant watching me go. I waved one last time, watched as they waved back, and rounded the corner.

I thought about the upcoming trip and being home for the holidays. Initially, the idea sounded wonderful, but as the time grew closer to leave, I felt hesitant. After a decade of being divorced, I had adapted to holidays being different, except Christmas. That one never came around without stomping on my heart a bit and leaving me melancholy. I longed to take us all back to the time when everyone was under one roof; we knew the traditions and joy of being a family. Snuggled in bed, the kids believed in Santa, and I believed, apparently, that life would always stay so simple!

Fifty-eight

I waited until a few minutes before five o'clock before leaving my apartment, out the enormous doors of the palazzo, on December 8, 2014. My taxi was already there in the early predawn hour to take me to the airport. I am continually amazed at the efficiency and promptness of the taxi service in Florence. It defies how the rest of the city operates!

Neither the driver nor I felt very chatty at that hour, and I only half listened to the news that was coming from the radio. My ears love the Italian language, even when I don't understand every word. The melodic lilt and flow of each sentence, the extended vowels, and rolling "R" sounds soothe me.

I settled into the backseat as we drove through the hushed darkness past the dimly lit apartment buildings and shops. In a few hours, all of them would come alive in a vibrancy that is uniquely Italian; horns would honk, espresso cups clatter, and a new day would begin in this ancient city. But I would not be part of it today.

I navigated my way just twenty minutes later through the doors of the airport and up the elevator to the check-in desk. Christmas gifts filled my suitcase, making it far too large for carry-on luggage. The beautiful woman behind the Air France desk asked for my passport, and we exchanged simple pleasantries. She asked me a few more questions, and I blankly gazed ahead, functioning on too little sleep and not enough caffeine.

"What?" I asked in English.

"I thought you spoke Italian," she shot back.

"Yeah, me too," I replied again in English, as I was not in the mood to argue with a beautiful Italian woman at this hour of the day.

The waiting area of Peretola, the Florence airport, is one large room and always crowded. I never understood why, when one has a seat on the plane, people feel the need to jump up and stand in line for twenty minutes before they board the plane, but many do. Ever the observer, I watched couples and families, and single travelers, and made up stories in my mind about who they were and where they were headed.

There was an air traffic controller strike at Charles de Gaulle, where I was making an early connection, so the majority of flights into Paris were cancelled. I hoped the early-morning trek to the airport I had just taken wouldn't result in taking a taxi right back to via di Mezzo to wait until tomorrow.

Once on the plane, we waited for forty-five minutes on the tarmac, as only a fraction of the planes were able to land in Paris. A young woman on a cell phone in the row ahead of me chatted away, much to the distress of the flight attendant, whom she persistently ignored. Tension grew among the passengers, as well as the flight crew, while the minutes dragged on and we all remained seated. Several times we received the word that we were ready for takeoff, only to remain stationary.

My scheduled hour and a half between flights in Paris was already cutting it close, and now I'd have under an hour to clear customs and board the flight to Salt Lake City.

As our clearance was given, flight attendant and chatting young woman about came to blows, we finally took off, leaving the early-morning light reflecting off of the terracotta rooftops of Florence.

Charles de Gaulle is an unforgiving airport if you aren't familiar with it. I made a beeline down the long halls and onto a bus, which meandered in a loop of circles or so it seemed, to the international gate. Crowds were sparse as so many flights had been cancelled, and I took off in a full sprint toward my gate. As I ran, another man sprinted beside me.

He asked if I was headed to Dallas, and I breathlessly said, "No, Salt Lake City!"

"I hope you make it," he yelled as he flew past me.

Eyeing my gate, my sprint became a fast walk as I saw the area was empty of travelers. Only one man remained at the desk, and two security gentlemen stood in front of the ramp, but I could see the plane through the window.

"I need to get on that flight," I said to them, in a voice filled with panic.

They asked me the usual questions of how long I'd been in Europe, and what the nature of my business had been here, and I told them, again, I really wanted to make the flight. We did a few more rounds of that, until their questions became less about my time in Europe, and more about why I was so adamant to make that particular flight. I backed off my urgency, sensing it was not helping my cause, and finally, one of them assured me he'd get me on my flight, but first, I was to answer their questions.

Total relief washed over me at hearing his words. I answered a few more questions, and he escorted me to the plane's door. I boarded the now-full plane, overheated in my layers of sweaters and scarves, but ready for a big glass of wine and another trip across the Atlantic Ocean.

Fifty-nine

As Delta flight #88 dropped down between the two mountain ranges that surround Salt Lake City, covered in a heavy blanket of snow, they looked like old friends to me, familiar in their imposing outline against the sky. I could close my eyes and see the outline of Mount Olympus and the peaks below it. I wore a silver ring on my finger called a Wasatch ring, which is the outline of those mountains, and more than anything else, they said "home" to me.

It was two o'clock in the afternoon, but I felt a fuzziness that only traveling through multiple time zones can bring. Not really awake, not tired, not really hungry, but not full.

Baggage claim was my first jolt back into life in the U.S., as the crowd seemed woefully underdressed and very loud. I knew what the American stereotype is, thanks to the candid conversations I'd had with my Italian and British friends, and right now, I agreed with them.

My children knew that my first night back would be an early one for me, and after our traditional take-out dinner of Indian food together, I would drop onto the futon in the guest bedroom in a heap at about seven-thirty p.m.

———

December nights in Utah are frigid, and waking up at two o'clock in the morning for the first week had me tiptoeing out to the living room to turn up the heat. I knew I wouldn't be able to go back to sleep, so I would plug in the Christmas lights and sit in the dark amid the twinkling lights with a steaming cup of coffee.

Lauren had decorated her small condo with some decorations from our past Christmases, but also with many things that were just hers. The few ornaments I had kept were buried deep inside a huge box, which was buried in a storage unit miles away; my memory strained in the dark stillness to remember what our Christmases had looked like years before.

I gazed at the tall wooden soldier that Lauren had placed by her tree. I'd always placed him in the same position—he commemorated Lauren's and my time in the *Nutcracker* ballet, where we both danced the part of the wooden soldier.

The advent calendar that used block numbers to count down the days to Christmas had been placed on the end table, but the numbers were woefully behind in their counting. It had always been my job to change the numbers, so I thought perhaps some things remained the same.

However, most everything does change, I surmised on those nights sitting alone in the oversized chair that had always been my favorite; life is about change, and the soul is about expansion, and only in growth do we find our truth, our purpose, and our courage.

Change and expansion had been key words in the last couple of years for me, and this was my third Christmas not having a home of my own for the holidays. Generally, I thrived in the freedom of not owning a home. I was thrilled to turn the key to lock the door on a rental apartment and be off on a new adventure. But Christmastime brought a renewed longing to me, to have a home to decorate and familiar possessions as well as people around me.

On those nights, where my only light was from the sliver of the moon and flickering reflections from the Christmas tree, I wondered what my Italian friends would think of Christmas in America.

I had talked to Donatella and Andrea about visiting me here. Andrea had been to the U.S. in the 1980s and driven through the Grand Canyon. Donatella had been to the East Coast when she was in her early twenties and said that was enough for her. I knew that she had a fear of flying, and when Donatella ended the conversation with her usual, "We'll see, my dear," I knew better than to press the issue.

I smiled to myself to picture my Italian companions in Utah! The rapid-paced, drive-through–everything, streamlined, fast-food life would leave them either in awe or horrified. I guessed it would be the latter.

I'd gone by a new CVS Pharmacy earlier in the day, where one could drive through to pick up a prescription. That would horrify Italians, as conversation, community, and waiting in line are key ingredients in picking up a prescription.

I winced at a memory of my visit to a *farmacia* in my first year in Florence, when I had asked the lady at the counter for a laxative. The Italian diet and I were not doing well together, and a trip to the pharmacy is the only way to buy any kind of medication. Aspirin, laxatives, pain relievers—which are readily available over the counter in the U.S.—must be purchased from a *farmacia* in Italy, under the sign of the green cross.

The pharmacist kept asking me to repeat my request, which I did with increasing volume. That seemingly invited two Italian women to jump in the conversation, and explanations and remedies abounded as to what I needed for my problem. While they discussed and argued which teas and foods were best for constipation, I quietly paid and slipped out the door. *Mamma mia.*

By the time the first stream of light would break over Mount Olympus and into the small kitchen of the condo, I had generally gone through the roster of all my Italian and expat friends. Lorenzo and Letizia, Ivan in Cortona, Donatella and Andrea, Fabrizio and Annamaria at Hotel Pierre, and my best girlfriends, Caitlin and Alexandra would already be well into their day by this hour, unaware of how my heart filled with memories of them.

I marveled at the perfect timing each one of my Italian friends had arrived in my life, and the doors that had been opened to me because I had met them. Deep in those sleepless nights, as I sat in the reflection of our Christmas tree, I often wished for a home and roots; but by morning's light, I'd fallen in love with my life, on both sides of the ocean, without a permanent address, all over again.

Sixty

You will never be completely at home again, because part of your heart always will be elsewhere. That is the price you pay for the richness of loving and knowing people in more than one place.

—Miriam Adeney

"Does it feel good to be home again?" one of my friends from high school asked as we gathered a group together for lunch after Christmas. I was amazed at these enduring friendships as I looked around the long table of beautiful women, many of whom I had known from middle school, and some from grade school.

I had, of course, answered yes, it did feel good to be here again, but the words stuck in my throat a bit before I was able to say them.

While I loved being in Salt Lake City at Christmastime with my children and surrounded by friends, I felt that I was visiting—I wasn't home. There was a soundtrack playing in the back of my mind, but it didn't fit with the video I was seeing with my eyes.

I missed Florence. I felt as though I'd left part of myself there, and while I was functioning in Utah, I was a beat behind. I missed the cacophony of music and noise that made up my daily life in Italy—the vibrancy of colors, food, and art, and the endless miles of walking I did each day. I missed what felt like home.

Sixteen months had passed since I'd last been in Utah. The changes that occurred during my second year in Italy had been monumental. These weren't the subtle workings of a tide, washing its way over rocks and gently forming softer edges. These changes had felt like an earthquake, the sudden jolt of the earth's mantle shifting, and left me to scramble for solid footing.

I had landed in Italy for the second year armed with a visa and living in a beautiful apartment overlooking the Bardini Garden. However, I'd also been betrayed by two men who sought to financially cripple me, and I stared down some of the darkest days in my life because of them.

In the sixteen months since then, I cofounded a tour company, been on *The Today Show*, and successfully carved out a new life in a foreign country. I was not the same woman I had been when I boarded a flight in September 2013, and certainly not the same woman who stood in a coffee shop in Rome in June 2012.

Life had handed me some serious highs and lows in the couple of years following my decision to move. Almost nothing had remained the same.

The one constant in all those months, however, was the love I carried in my heart. Love had carried me out of a dark corner in San Niccolò when I questioned whether I had the strength to go on. I'd felt the force of love from friends and family I couldn't see and hadn't the energy to talk to, and from the angels I sensed around me.

Love overflowed now that I was here in Utah again. It was tangible as I met with the loyal and lifelong friends who had supported me from across the ocean, and two children who cheered me on and embraced my vision of a new life. It felt good to hug these precious people, who, while they could not visualize the life I led now half a world away, still encouraged me.

"You're just like the lady in that book *Eat, Pray, Love,*" was a common comment.

"Yes," I would think to myself, "but I remained in the land of *Eat*!"

"You're just like the lady in that movie…what was it? *Under the Tuscan Sun*!"

"Yes," I would answer for the thousandth time. It was easier to agree than try to explain.

My life was not at all like Elizabeth Gilbert's or Francis Mayes's, or Julia Roberts's or Diane Lane's for that matter! While I admired all of those women, there was no book advance to see me through a year of traveling. I had no husband, no home, and no financial parachute of any kind. I was living my life, not telling a story, in a foreign country, and my day-to-day life didn't seem much like the movies.

The one common thread I did feel with those women was our passion for the beauty of Italy. The inspiration that had led Dante to write, Michelangelo to carve the white marble of Carrara, and more recently, the Carletti family to make remarkable wine is in the air. I understand the magic that Tuscany has held for women; I breathe it in my daily life, in the markets and in the museums, and it has left an indelible mark on my soul.

Passion stirred in me now, on both sides of the ocean, to continue moving toward this new, internal calling. I had never lived smaller, had less money, or been so alone, and yet I was enthusiastic about each day. I visualized and meditated, opened my mind and heart to new answers.

As Wayne Dyer often counseled, I strove to have a mind open to everything but attached to nothing. I had seen myself through the eyes of another culture and been the outsider. I'd been the minority, the one who didn't know the rules, or the way, or the words.

It had humbled me, finding my way to a life in Florence, but it also strengthened me in a way I'd never experienced before. In an unforgiving climate that belies its exterior, Florence gave me some harsh lessons. She held up a mirror and required me to know myself. But the result of surviving the lessons, and ultimately flourishing in that city, now made it feel like home. I missed her.

In these past two years, I had given myself the gift of time and space to come to know my own heart, my own intentions, my weaknesses, and my own truth. I now know that joy is in direct proportion to living one's truth, as the masters of wisdom have always taught, and as 2014 came to an end, I knew I was living mine.

Sixty-one

I had to visit the doctor while I was in Utah, as I had found a lump in my breast. After being weighed and having my blood pressure checked, I found myself worrying more about the new number on the scale than the lump.

"I can't believe I've gained almost eight pounds," I lamented to Lelan, who was not only a lifelong friend, but a nurse. I felt safe telling her the new number that had upped me into an all-time high, save for my pregnancies.

"You look beautiful," she said, as all good girlfriends around the world would reply. But she even added, "I think you look better, in fact. A little softness on our faces is a good thing at our age."

My mind flashed to one of my favorite scenes in *Eat, Pray, Love*, when Julia Roberts asks her friend, over margherita pizza in Naples, if any man had ever walked out when she undressed. Once they agreed that, no, muffin tops seemed more bothersome to the women who have them than the men who hold them, they finished eating the pizza and decided to buy bigger jeans!

I realized it had been a couple of years since I'd been with a man, and the freedom of not worrying about if my body was desirable or not was a new experience. I no longer stood in front of groups to teach fitness classes on a daily basis and had felt no pressure to maintain a certain weight or size.

"How much are you walking each day?" Lelan asked, in nurse mode now.

When I told her I was walking at least five miles a day, especially when I was in Florence, and that I felt healthy, she gave me the kindest advice of all.

"Then relax. Your body likes being this weight, you look beautiful, and you can walk through Florence and hike through the Cinque Terre." And then she added, "Worry about bigger things if you want to worry."

I thought about her comment as I looked at myself in the mirror. My face *was* softer, gentler than it had been in my younger, low-fat years. My heart was softer too. In releasing the stringent bar of perfection for myself I had released my expectation of it in others as well.

I thought of my neighborhood in Florence, where I lived in the Borgo Pinti area, and the diverse, international people who shared markets, streets, and shops with me. It was impossible to be judgmental in the potpourri of races, languages, and dress that each group brought to the mix. I missed that diversity in Utah, one of the most homogenized states in the U.S.

> *Be soft. Do not let the world make you hard. Do not let pain make you hate. Do not let the bitterness steal your sweetness.*
>
> —Kurt Vonnegut

Lao Tzu made a similar statement in the *Tao Te Ching*: *Be soft, like water. Water is fluid, soft, and yielding. But water will wear away rock, which is rigid and cannot yield.*

Perhaps that is a lesson in growing older—be softer, more approachable, less opinionated, and thereby not so easily offended. I had lived among other cultures for the past two years, and that had shown me, as Richard had told me, there are many ways to reach L.A.

The doctor I saw wasn't overly concerned about the lump I had in my breast but did want to do some further tests. That meant a longer stay in Utah than I had planned, and my three weeks would be seven.

January in freezing cold Utah is not my idea of a good time, but Delta changed my ticket without a hassle, and I notified Lorenzo of my change in plans. I asked him if he would go into my apartment and water the plants and check that everything was okay, and he wrote back immediately that he would.

Lelan lent me an extra car that she had, an SUV, which I would need in January to drive in the snow and ice. That helped my attitude immensely, and I realized another month in Utah would mean lunches with my high school girlfriends, more time with the Dodo girls, a trip to Albuquerque to see Shauna and, of course, unhurried time with Lauren and Justin.

Justin's schedule was flexible, and so we would often meet downtown for coffee and the *New York Times* crossword puzzle. The Rose Establishment was his new favorite for morning coffee and quickly became mine as well. It was exciting to see new, hip places where locals of all ages came together in Salt Lake. It had the feel of the coffee bars in Florence, Ditta Artigianale and Rifrullo, and helped me ease into a longer stay.

Justin and I would whip through the puzzle from Mondays to Thursdays, cry over the harder Friday and Saturday versions, and generally love the Sundays. I realized how precious these days were, every day doing simple things with people I cherished. I had spent so much time alone, with just my own thoughts for company, that this closeness was a welcome change.

By the time I was given a clean bill of health, I'd moved into a daily routine in Utah, even in January, with surprising ease. During the frigid, gray days, I worked on the spring tour preparations, corresponding with the ladies for their trip ahead, and wrote for *Huffington Post*.

At night, as I drifted off to sleep, in my mind I would visit Florence. I had walked every street so many times and knew where the colorful- graffiti was, each ornate doorknob and lamppost. I knew where there were stones missing in the cobblestone paths and who would have laundry hanging out the window.

I'd visualize the zigzagged path up to the top of the Bardini Garden and the breathless view it would provide me once I was there. I could see in my mind the gorgeous burst of violet color and fragrance that the hyacinth arch held in the early spring, and the view out to the terracotta domes of the Duomo and Medici Chapels.

I'd come to know the people in my neighborhood and wondered if they noticed I hadn't been by. The lady who owns the beauty shop along Borgo Pinti, who waves back at me as I go by now, Fabrizio at *The Box,* where I'd often stop to try out a new wine, or the *fruttivendolo* at Sant'Ambrogio who would always comment that I didn't *have* to cook alone…did they notice I was gone?

I knew the song of Florence. I wondered if Florence knew my song, missed me walking her ancient streets, and if she knew that I'd be back.

Sixty-two

Grief is a most peculiar thing; we're so helpless in the face of it. It's like a window that will simply open of its own accord. The room grows cold, and we can do nothing but shiver. But it opens a little less each time, and a little less; and one day we wonder what has become of it.

—Arthur Golden

There is more sky in New Mexico than anywhere else I have ever seen. Like a big azure dome that covers the entire stratosphere, I am always taken aback by how massive the western sky is! The clouds in the day and stars of the night make watching the sky a major attraction of Albuquerque to me.

The only other attraction there, for me, is my dear friend Shauna, and I wanted to make the short side trip to see her while I was in Utah.

Shauna and I spent a few days together in the frigid month of January and drove up to one of my favorite cities in the U.S., Santa Fe. The clouds formed long silvery fingers through the sky as the rays of sun broke through, and I tried to take pictures through the windshield as Shauna drove us along the highway.

I have a weakness for anyone who can make me laugh. I will forgive a host of bad qualities if you take me to the place of funny, where, without a moment's hesitation, I laugh! And the best person I know for doing just that is Shauna Offret.

Shauna made me laugh that day, as she had for over twenty-five years. She has the amazing ability to quickly sum up a situation in its most ridiculous terms! We were famous for laughing together at inappropriate times, through classes, parties, and a thousand lunches with what I call the "church giggles," and today was no different.

We had initially met when I was teaching aerobics at a local recreation center where she worked out lifting weights. She is the yin to my yang. To my endless amazement, she can fix a roof, rip out the roots of a dead tree, and bake banana bread all in one day. But mostly, she can make me laugh.

Shauna moved to Albuquerque to be by her family in 2006, a particularly rough year for me, so our conversations continued daily for that first year. Since I'd been in Italy, we would schedule a Skype call every week or so, and both of us knew that would mean at least two hours together. She, too, had recently gone through a divorce after thirty-plus years of marriage. But after we'd covered the basics, what was new, and how the kids were, we would find the funny. She would always leave my heart feeling lighter and my stomach aching from laughter.

Life had picked both of us up and set us down in scenarios neither of us could have planned, but we had always had each other. As I hugged her goodbye at the airport to return to Salt Lake City, and ultimately Florence, I hated to let go. Both of us held on a little longer and then started to cry. "I just don't like that you're so far away," she often told me. Gone were the days when she was just up the road, at the gym, or dropping by with a large diet cola for each of us.

It felt so good to laugh with Shauna during a couple of gray days in January, to look into her warm brown eyes and see my old friend's spirit start to return. She is my friend with whom there just never is enough time. We had been known to sit on a porch for hours, sometimes holding hands, just talking and laughing.

Like most transitions in life, I couldn't remember the exact time when I had started smiling and laughing again. There had been dark days when I was convinced it would never happen, and yet, it had. I had needed time, and distance, and had given myself a good bit of both.

Maybe grief never leaves completely, but I do know it changes until it finally becomes bearable. Much like the scars I see on my body that are well healed from time now, they are no longer too tender to touch, but just gentle reminders of where I have been and what I have been through.

Back in Salt Lake City, my huge suitcase remained open for the last few days, as it always does toward the end of a stay. I tried to solve the puzzle of making everything fit, determining what to place in carry-on (in case the big suitcase took a separate trip), what to take back to Florence, and what to leave behind or give away.

I marveled at how life was so easy in the U.S. For the first few weeks back, it always sped by in a blur, too streamlined and overwhelming. But I knew the steps to this dance, and it was natural to eventually fall back into the rhythm of life in Utah.

I had learned my lesson about winter months in Florence last year, so I sealed my full-length down parka in an airtight plastic bag, trying to minimize its bulky size. With the hood pulled up, it couldn't be less attractive. I looked like the Michelin man wrapped in black tires rolling down the narrow streets of Borgo Pinti, but I gave up the *bella figura* once the frigid, humid winter months arrived in Florence.

Inside my apartment, the ancient plastered walls held in the damp cold, and without a bathtub and with limited hot water for a shower, I knew this coat was my best defense for the next month or so and worth the space it occupied in my suitcase.

Aveda shampoo and conditioner, Clinique makeup, washcloths, Eclipse gum, and almond butter always make the trip from the U.S., along with a few small gifts for my Italian friends. I hadn't brought many clothes, as this had started out to be just a three-week trip, so packing for the return trip was fairly easy.

I looked out at the snow-covered ground from the large windows of the living room in Lauren's condo and tried to imagine my neighborhood of Borgo Pinti. I wondered if the graffiti still covered the yellow paint outside the large doors to the courtyard, where someone named Antonio had declared his undying love to Vittoria.

As much as I looked forward to catching up with Alexandra and the Gucci girls, Georgette and Nardia, it stung a little to leave Utah again. I couldn't wait to set off on a day's adventure through the Chianti countryside with Andrea and Donatella, but I had loved the lazy mornings of crossword puzzles and coffee with Justin and evening dinners with Lauren.

I sat in the comfort of my favorite floral chair, the cushions worn by my familiar frame, and realized the grief I had felt when in Utah had abated some. I no longer wanted to quickly arrive and depart, but a light had cracked through to soften the darkness here, and without my being aware, allowed me to exhale…in Utah.

Twenty-one women were counting on my return to Florence, as the March and April tours of Tuscany were both full. They would be making a trip of a lifetime to Italy, and I was happily making preparations to share my new home with them.

As I closed the top of my suitcase, I was ready. I was ready for the long flight, the discomfort, the hassle that is Charles de Gaulle airport but, ultimately, the descent into the small Tuscan city, my beloved home, Florence.

Sixty-three

With an enormous suitcase and some difficulty, I had said goodbye to Salt Lake City, my friends, and my children—again. I wondered, certainly not for the first time that day, if I was crazy to go. The pulling away always felt the same, and after three years, it hadn't become any easier—only more difficult.

In previous visits, when I had dropped into Salt Lake City for two or three weeks, it had seemed like a mini vacation away from my usual life. But the almost two months I'd spent this time had washed the rituals of Italy off me it seemed, and I had slipped easily into my American life.

As I waited in the long security line of the Salt Lake City airport, I tried to visualize a sunset over the Arno and the melodic chaos of my favorite market in Sant'Ambrogio. I tried to remember the sights and sounds of my small apartment in Borgo Pinti that had been waiting seven weeks for my return.

I boarded the plane for the long haul across the ocean with my mind still clinging to the hugs from my children. They were always aware of how difficult leaving becomes for me on the last day, and so we switch roles. They reminded me of how brave I was, and what an inspiration I was to them, and I allowed them to see how vulnerable I felt.

Reluctant inspiration, I thought as I settled into my window seat and took in the final view of the snow-capped Rocky Mountains. My ancestors left Denmark, walked across the United States to come through the canyon in those mountains to live their lives in Utah. I was headed back to Europe, separating myself, yet again, from the valley they had settled.

Almost twenty-four hours later (thirty-two with the time change), I arrived in Florence, Italy. Lorenzo had come by to water and set my plants out in the corridor to get some sun after I'd notified him of my delay in returning. I walked to my apartment door, under the bust of the ever-watchful Dante, and looked down at them. They looked how I felt: dreary and exhausted.

The apartment in Borgo Pinti was freezing cold! While it rarely snows in Florence, the winter months are cold with a damp chill that attaches to my bones and won't let go. I dropped the suitcases on the Oriental carpet of vibrant reds and blues, and walked through my place. It seemed alien to me, devoid of any sound or any energy. I turned on the heat and opened the cupboard to see if there was anything to eat.

I was so hungry, but the cupboards were almost bare, save a few stale crackers, some coffee, and a bottle of Brunello wine that Fabrizio had given to me for a Christmas gift. From my suitcase I dragged out a jar of almond butter, which had made the voyage intact, opened the wine, and that, on a few stale crackers, would be dinner.

A few bites and less than five minutes later, the power blew. "Welcome back to Florence," I thought, wearily. It never failed.

I hadn't paid for January minutes on my Italian cell phone, so I had no phone and now no Internet. I trudged across town and prayed Lorenzo was home, grateful that no one who refers to me as their inspiration could see me now.

Lorenzo opened the door and exuberantly kissed my cheeks and welcomed me back! He had me sit down in his kitchen while he changed into some walking shoes and grabbed his coat. As he returned, he looked at my weary face and smiled.

"*Non preoccuparti, cara,*" Lorenzo said, telling me not to worry. He took my arm and linked it through his as we briskly set out into the dusk of Florence.

Lorenzo did a quick check of the apartment, went out to the power box, and within minutes, had restored light and heat to my place. He explained that he'd left the hot water heater on in the bathroom so I would be able to take a shower upon arrival, and when I'd turned the heat on for the apartment, the fragile ecosystem that is power in Florence said no.

He declined my offer of some really good wine with stale crackers and told me I'd see him later in the week when he'd come by to collect the rent money. As I walked with him to the outside corridor, Lorenzo asked if I'd noticed the motion light he had installed over my front door while I was gone. I had and thanked him for that and also for having the hall light in the foyer replaced.

Lorenzo assured me that Margherita had been by the apartment to change the linens on my bed, and fresh towels awaited me in the bathroom. I felt my gloom lift a bit in the presence of my first Italian friend. He was always in motion, in a hurry, but while he maintained three phones and a dozen apartments, he was never too busy to help me.

I know this to be an eternal truth about traveling—twelve hours of sleep does wonders for a tired soul! And so it did for me.

I stepped out the next day into Florence for the first time since my long absence from my neighborhood. I stopped at my favorite *fruttivendolo* and then the grocery store. I wanted to recapture the familiarity of my city, so I detoured from the store and walked across the piazza of Santa Croce. As I did, I heard the sweet sound of a violin playing.

I reveled in the luxury of being almost alone in this famous square, which sits in front of the largest Franciscan church in the world. *Florence rewards her year-round citizens with days such as these!* I thought, as I gazed up at the alabaster white of the church against the blue sky of Tuscany. The magnificence of Santa Croce, with its enormous statue of Dante, began to warm my heart, and my steps quickened.

Recognizable now, as I approached the violin player, was the familiar melody of *Let It Be*. The music filled my ears and then my soul. The initial joy I had experienced in Italy began to pump through my veins again, and I felt it rise up to my chest.

It had been a journey to find more joy that led me to take a gigantic leap of faith and settle here in my beloved Florence. It was imagining this kind of vision that made the sale of my home and worldly possessions seem sensible. Now, as I moved through my third year, I could feel love for both countries without knowing for sure which one was home.

I did not always feel courageous. I would wallow in reluctant inspiration on occasion and miss both Utah and Tuscany when I left them. I would long for the people whom I loved on both sides of the ocean, and I hated saying goodbye.

But the ache and longing would only last for a small amount of time as I would become absorbed into the life I had in each country. I had found my life's work and passion straddling both cultures. And, as Mother Mary whispered words of wisdom on that day, I let it be.

Sixty-four

Once the initial sting of separating from Utah was over, I settled back into my life in Florence. It was almost as though I hadn't been gone, as everyone had been busy with Christmas and now, in the days of February, my girlfriends had time for leisurely lunches.

Alexandra stayed heavily booked in the tourist months, so I would often go for a couple of weeks without seeing her except to wave on the street while she was giving a tour! During my tours, she would give the initial introduction to Florence with a walking tour of the city, and occasionally join us in Cortona, but other than that, work season for us meant not seeing each other much and settling for morning chats on the phone.

Now we had time to catch up on new restaurants, museum exhibits, and life in general. I had become good friends with the British artist Elizabeth Orchard, who creates not only large canvas paintings, but also paints on silk scarves. Georgette and Nardia continued to expand their own networks and businesses as two of the most sought-after social media strategists in the city.

Without the crowds of tourists and tour season, we all had the time to slow down a bit before the next season began, and long lunches where we lingered over a tiramisu and coffee were delicious.

One chilly Saturday afternoon, Alexandra led a walking tour to Fratelli Piccini, one of the oldest jewelry stores on the Ponte Vecchio. This exquisite shop survived the bombs around the bridge during World War II and the flood of 1966, when the water of the Arno rose right to the top of the shop.

During the tour we had amazing access to not only pieces of priceless jewelry, but the priceless views of the Uffizi Gallery and directly below to the Arno River as well. Looking out from the jewelry store workshop, squeezed between the Vasari Corridor and the salesroom, I asked myself a now-familiar question: "How in the world did *I* get here?"

Alexandra needed to practice her tour of San Marco for a tour later in the week, so she asked Nardia, Georgette, and me if we wanted to meet her there for what would surely be a magnificent afternoon among the frescoes of Fra Angelico.

I was somewhat familiar with this former convent, now a museum, where Girolamo Savonarola had lived, and Fra Angelico had painted a fresco in each of the monk's cells. Cosimo de' Medici even had a cell for his personal retreat, and many paintings remain, including Angelico's most famous, and utterly moving, *The Annunciation*.

To live among such gorgeous works of art had changed me in a tangible way. I had come to understand the meanings in the artwork, the symbols and colors of the Renaissance masters. I watched the young schoolchildren on their field trips to some of the most famous galleries in the world and wondered what it would have been like to grow up in Italy.

As I left the girls, I wrapped my heavy woolen scarf up higher to protect me from the damp cold. I thought about the decades of my life that preceded this one and seemed like separate lifetimes strung out behind me. I am happy to walk alone along the back streets of Borgo Pinti, weave in and out of the maze that I have figured out is the shortest path to my apartment. I look forward to the solitary hours that will follow, a quiet dinner alone, maybe some reading.

I remember a story though of a young student who asked his teacher for a butterfly after seeing them in his teacher's garden.

The teacher gave the young student a chrysalis instead, explaining the magic of the change from caterpillar to butterfly.

For days the student intently watched the chrysalis for the miracle to occur, and finally, a small dot appeared in the chrysalis where the now-butterfly started to emerge.

But the process seemed slow to the young student and, peering into the growing opening of the chrysalis, the student urged the butterfly to come out. Finally, when the suspense became unbearable, the young student enlarged the opening, afraid the butterfly was stuck and would never emerge.

Of course, the ending of this story was a painful lesson, as hurrying the process along had killed, not aided, the butterfly. As the teacher pointed out to the disappointed student, sometimes the best help we give someone, or something, is to allow them to find their own way, in their own timing.

I had lived decades where not much had changed—being a wife, mother, and fitness teacher had spanned three of them. Finding my way now, in my own timing, was occasionally lonely, made difficult by distance and a different culture, but I wouldn't have changed a thing about it. I could feel I was working my way through some necessary growth, and I sensed that was the purpose of my being here.

My story seemed to strike a chord with many who were seeking change in their lives and wondered what was next for them.

I had met a lady for a coffee who had written to me after reading some of my articles on *Huffington Post*. I thought she was just visiting Florence because she loved the city. As we talked, she told me of her daughter who had been to school here, and then her eyes met mine.

"Does she live in the U.S. now?" I asked her, innocently.

"She died. I lost her," she answered, her tears now overflowing.

I didn't look away or change the subject. I just took her hand. I didn't know, thank God, that kind of grief, but I knew enough.

Grief makes people uncomfortable, as though the event that led to it may be contagious. But I have come to know that when we sit with another, when we just hold that sacred space of sharing their pain, we give the greatest gift of all. We give our humanity, and our love.

I read through the names of the ladies who would be arriving in the March and April tours. They all told me a little bit about themselves, and many were recent widows. One told me her husband was killed in an accident, and she witnessed his death. She booked the trip for her daughter and herself before the holidays, as she'd wanted them to have something to look forward to. I am honored she chose to see Tuscany with me, and I was humbled by her courage.

Sixty-five

I was standing on the corner of via Calimala and via de'Lamberti, waiting for the arrival of another lady for the March tour. A couple from the group had already arrived and opted, in their jet-lagged fog, to head to their rooms for a nap.

I looked up from my phone as a taxi squealed around the corner and laughed to see the woman in the backseat pointing at me and waving madly! Tanya from Texas!

I felt like I already knew Tanya Pierce, a woman on the March tour, as we had corresponded via email quite a bit. I could tell by her writing that she was pure Texan, larger than life with a heart to match. She had sent each of the women in the group an email telling them how excited she was to share an adventure with them and asking a prayer of safety on them all. I have no idea how she found this particular tour, or me, but I couldn't wait to meet her!

She gave me a big, Texas hug hello, and when I asked her if she wanted to check in and rest for a bit, she said absolutely not! She was ready to see Florence!

The details of arranging and delivering the welcome bags to Hotel Pierre for the group had taken more time than I thought they would. I had planned to get to the bustling Sant'Ambrogio market that morning to buy fruit for the week, but I hadn't made it there. I asked Tanya if she wanted a brisk twenty-minute walk out of the center of Florence, promising lunch at the end. She agreed.

I have a fondness for anyone who can walk as fast as I do. Dalliers and slow walkers are pet peeves of mine, and I usually have to remind myself when walking with a tour group to slow down. In their defense, they are sightseeing and window shopping, and I am usually on a mission, which requires full-speed-ahead action! Tanya matched me step for step, even as we chatted and became acquainted. The cobblestones and crowds of people didn't slow her down a bit.

As we headed down via del Corso, Tanya told me she had spent her career as a U.S. Justice Department attorney. That sounded impressive already, but by the time we sat down to lunch and began swapping stories, I was charmed by this Texas belle. Her life had been exciting, and one of service. Tanya's manner was pure Southern charm, and it turned out I was slightly less charmed than the owner of Rocco's Trattoria, who kept coming by for a hug and peck on the cheek! Throughout the very typical Tuscan lunch, where we sat at communal tables, he was most attentive!

There were a couple of ladies from Salt Lake City who were coming on this tour—Lisa Jerome and Kim Butterfield. They were each coming with family members: Lisa with her sister Lyne Deleo-Burks, and Kim with her cousin and niece. Sarah was to arrive later in the day, and the ladies were all familiar with her as she was the local contact in the U.S. and the one sending them their Welcome Packets.

I was always thrilled and nervous on the first day of the tours. I wanted everyone to arrive, with luggage, on time, and safely. The "safely" part always happened, but delayed flights and lost luggage were a reoccurring theme!

"It flows in Italy like rain in England," Antonio from La Bussola would always tell the ladies as he filled their glasses with *prosecco*. I'm not sure if he remembered that these ladies were from the United States, not England, but it didn't matter. If *prosecco* was flowing, the ladies were smiling, and after several glasses and a full pizza from La Bussola later, they were ready for bed.

Like a mother hen, I was always relieved when every lady arrived safely. They would never be able to anticipate fully the week ahead and all that they would see and experience, but I knew. As I walked to my apartment in Borgo Pinti, rounded past the Duomo and turned up via dell'Oriuolo, I looked up at the cream-colored moon hanging low in the inky sky. My heart was full of anticipation of the week ahead, and gratitude. I was aware that to numb my pain was to numb my joy to the same level, and so I had chosen not to. I had chosen to crack my heart wide open, and on this night I felt my heart deeply satisfied in the present moment. I was living in Florence, Italy, and a beautiful new group of ladies had been tucked into their hotel, and now, I was walking home thinking I might be the luckiest girl in the world.

Sixty-six

Six days after the March tour had begun, I was seated on the cool steps of the town hall in Cortona under the clock tower made famous in *Under the Tuscan Sun*. The hub of this small hill town was bustling on a Saturday with its citizens and tourists alike. The open market was in full swing in Piazza Signorelli, just above this square, alive with bursts of color, noise, and locals buying everything from cheese to bathrobes in one spot. Several ladies in the tour group were part of the crowd in the market as well, as they found it necessary to purchase an extra piece of luggage in order to get all their purchases back to the U.S.! I had warned them that Tuscany is a shopper's paradise!

I watched as some of the group headed to the *alimentari* to have a *panino* made, and others were off to Il Mondo di Amelie, a small boutique shop next to the Teatro Signorelli, filled with gorgeous Umbrian linen, dishes, and scented soaps. The shop owner, Valentina, and her mother, Alba, fussed over each lady in my group and sneaked in a soap or lotion gift with every purchase. Their kindness was classic small-town Tuscany, and I had come to adore both of them.

We had spent part of the morning with Ivan Botonici, who had prepared a spread of warm focaccia bread topped with his own olive oil and various patés. The "rain of Italy," *prosecco*, had accompanied the food as well, and after almost a week here none of the ladies thought it odd to be offered alcohol before noon!

Ivan had given our group a tour of his shop, Il Pozzo, which he had originally purchased not realizing there was an ancient well inside the space. He excavated an old pilgrimage hostel where people and animals shared the space on their way to Rome. Ivan had also generously shared the details of the history of Cortona with the Etruscan walls dating back to the eighth century B.C. and made it come to life for the group.

As I stood to the side surrounded by walls with luscious paintings and photographs, I looked at each one of the women in this tour. Their faces were glowing with relaxation and enjoyment, and then I looked at my friend, Ivan, and was thrilled to my core. *This* is what I had dreamt of a mere ten months ago! Here was the consummation of my hopes and all the plans for sharing Tuscany with women, and their eyes told me they realized a few of their dreams of Tuscany as well.

The time together seemed longer than just six days, and through that time the ladies each shared how they had found the tour and how they had known it was the one for them.

The morning of my feature on *The Today Show*, Tanya Pierce had taken her first sick day in years. She decided that day she was coming on a spring tour. Lisa Jerome, a former student of mine in Salt Lake City, had surprised her sister with a Christmas gift by bringing her to Tuscany. Lisa's generous spirit had spilled over to the entire group, and the two sisters were a source of upbeat fun and great energy.

Between day trips, shopping, eating, and hiking the trails of the Cinque Terre, these ladies forged a trust and a bond of friendship. Over steaming plates of pasta and glasses of Chianti, they shared their stories, joys, and sorrows alike.

I was honored to hear their stories and to be a catalyst to create a climate where they felt comfortable to share them. Later that night, our last night together, I would share my story with them in a class about courage, passion, and joy. And then, we would all have dinner at La Grotta, my favorite restaurant in Cortona, where Mariano had told me to go on my first trip here, and where I had toasted (to myself) the new business idea.

The clouds covered the early afternoon sun, and I drew my scarf around my neck, contented to sit on the steps of the town hall and watch a scene play out in front of my eyes as I guessed it had for centuries. Young children chased each other around the square, and the old men found their way to the bench directly across from me. Their manner with each other, and those who walked by, told me this was familiar, this was home to them. I had witnessed an almost identical scene each time I had visited Cortona, and I wondered how it felt to have stayed in a small town for one's entire life—the town of your parents and their parents, your children and their children. Do they think it is odd that an American woman has left her home across the ocean to make a life among them?

The arrival of a group of teenagers who took over the steps signaled my time to depart and head down via Nazionale to check on the ladies. I set my hand down to push off when something white caught my eye. A perfect feather, right next to my fingertip, signaled to me as always. I was on the right path.

Sixty-seven

"What would you do if you found out you had just six months to live?"

"What would you do if you won the lottery?"

"What would you do if you knew you could not fail?"

Each member of the group arrived for our last class together before we would leave for dinner in Cortona. They were dressed up tonight, their faces having been kissed by the Tuscan sun and their eyes sparkling as they found seats and set their notebooks and glasses of wine down. There was excitement in our last night together as a group and also a little sadness.

I asked each one to write the answers to those three questions, and then carefully study what they had written. Hidden in the written words were a life's longing, dreams, and adventures yet to be taken.

The three questions were what I had asked myself, essentially, in the small coffee shop in Rome in 2012. What was it I was longing to do before my life was over, irrespective of money or possibility of failure? My answer to all three, at that time, was the same—move to Italy.

Together we spoke of passion, living life wholeheartedly, and how to live independently of others' opinions. I talked about the gifts of intuition and inspiration and the roles they can play in daily life.

Together, as women have done since the beginning of time, we nurtured each other's dreams and cheered each other on.

By the time class was over and our five-course dinner ended at La Grotta, a tired but contented group of women headed down the crooked street of via Nazionale.

I climbed the creamy white steps to the third floor of Villa Marsili to my luxurious room of soft peach and apricot colors. Beautiful antiques, silky sheets, and a view of Val di Chiana below made this hotel something out of every woman's dreams. But for me, the best part of my room tonight was the bathtub, and before I headed to bed, I soaked in warm water and heavily scented bubbles. A bath was such a rare event in Italy, and my body was longing for the relaxation.

My bed had been turned down, pillows fluffed, and the inexplicable rug covers placed on the floor next to it. I wrapped up in the heavy terrycloth robe, slipped into my slippers that read "Villa Marsili" in emerald green, and walked to the window.

The little town of Camucia twinkled in lights below, and an absolute stillness permeated the valley. This was in stark contrast to Florence, which seemed to erupt to life around ten p.m. I could barely make out the dim outline of Santa Maria delle Grazie, the domed church, and the meandering road lined with cypress trees that twisted and curved until it reached Cortona.

The hush over the valley echoed the quiet contentment in my heart. It had been a successful tour with the ladies. I sensed they were deeply satisfied, and I had loved being with them. The next day, we would visit Le Celle, Santa Margherita church, and, of course, Bramasole, and then return to Florence where some would catch a flight, some a train, and some would stay for one more night.

"Good night," I whispered to the valley below, closing the heavy windows, and then I said the same to the ghosts of Villa Marsili, as surely there were a few.

Andrea had two trips to Cortona before noon the next morning, as one of the ladies had an early-morning flight out of Florence, an hour and a half away. Ludmila would leave Cortona by five a.m. and the rest of us at eleven. Ludmila Leontieva was a college professor and had just the days of her spring break off. She would be back in the classroom come Monday morning.

Ludmila had found my writing on *Huffington Post* and been following me since the very first piece had been published. She spoke with such a slight accent that it was hard to believe English wasn't her native language and Russian was. Her humor and generous heart had made her a favorite of the group, and of mine.

We had tried to say our goodbyes the night before but found it too difficult. I told her to tap on my door before she left in the morning so I could give her a hug, but she said she didn't think she could do that without tears. So, we agreed to not say goodbye…we would meet down the road, someplace, sometime.

Sixty-eight

The absolute peace and quiet of my apartment was a welcome cocoon where I wrapped myself up for a few days following a tour. The thick plaster walls offered a tomb-like relief from the noise and bustle of the jam-packed days of traveling in a pack of women, and I loved being home! Another tour group was to arrive in a week, and so my craving for solitude had to be satisfied.

I wondered when the transition had completed and I had become completely comfortable living alone. I hadn't realized how much time I spent in silence until it had been so limited. Now the quiet recharged me as did the piano music of Yiruma that I played each morning and the familiar sounds of my neighborhood that poured through my open windows.

Sarah had stayed for just five days of the last tour, as she wanted to spend her birthday with friends and family in the States. She wouldn't come back for the next tour, and I understood. Sarah was a mother of two young children, a wife, and an ever-seeking entrepreneur of new ideas and companies.

After a few days alone with the last group, I was confident I would be all right leading the next group by myself. Florence was home to me, and sharing my city with others was a comfortable role that energized me.

I made the rounds to the companies, shops, and restaurants that we would visit with the next group—bought tickets, paid bills, and generally maintained my friendships with these people whom I relied on throughout the tour. My head would be buzzing with a thousand details, but my mantra was *Slow down, small talk before money talk, slow down*…repeat. I knew the relationships with these people were key to the tour's success, and I frequently had to remind myself that this business was on Italian terms, not mine.

———

The new group arrived that April, and as always, I didn't know how they would gel and what the personalities of the group would be, but the serendipity would always present itself.

On the first of our two nights with Chef Leonardo preparing our dinner, the theme began to emerge. Out of the eleven women who had chosen this tour, five were recent widows. As they shared their stories, I could see the connections form. The golden light from the chandelier lit our private dining room and their faces. Music rose up to the third level of Hotel Pierre, where open windows looked out to the busy street below and across to the Orsanmichele church, which looked close enough to touch.

This was a gentle group who savored the experiences of art and architecture in Tuscany. They seemed to quickly assimilate and sense the others' personalities, and while four ladies had been college friends, two were mother–daughter and five were solo travelers. It had all the makings of creating a strange stew, but it didn't.

The daughter and youngest member of the group was Jen Baguley, whom I had known in Salt Lake City. She'd taken my Pilates classes from the time she was in high school, and I'd watched her get married, get her degree, and have two boys. I was thrilled to have her join me here, as well as her mom, Cindy Poulsen.

Cindy had a life-threatening infection several years prior, and had been given a fifty-fifty chance of surviving the necessary surgery. In the hospital, she had told Jen that one of her biggest regrets was that she had never seen Italy. Jen promised her an Italian vacation to take her mind off of the pain, and she instructed her mom to get better. As Cindy introduced herself to the other ladies, she let them know she was on her, "I-didn't-die tour of Italy!"

We all relied on Jen's technical knowledge to get the group's cell phones connected to the Internet, download Dropbox, and upload photos. By the end of the tour, she seemed to gather a few more mothers.

The stack of receipts on my kitchen table taunted me as I looked at them from across the room. Two tours, with just a week in between, had meant little sleep and no time for paperwork. The business part of the business now needed attention. Every charge, cash transaction, or ATM withdrawal during the whirlwind days of the tour, was waiting to be recorded and added up. I had the feeling that we had done better than just breaking even on these tours, so I poured myself a large glass of Madrone di Lohsa from Poliziano, compliments of Jennifer Criswell, and dove into the task at hand.

Sixty-nine

> *Your work is going to fill a large part of your life, and the only way to be truly satisfied is to do what you believe is great work. And the only way to do great work is to love what you do.*
>
> —Steve Jobs

There's no shortage of inspirational quotes on pursuing one's dreams and running one's own company. What generally is left out of those beautiful quotes is that you will probably work for about two cents an hour in the beginning! At least, that was what I thought as I stumbled to bed, bleary eyed at two o'clock after a night of accounting.

I refrained from being brutally honest to the several emails a week I received asking me if I needed an assistant! I knew it looked like a dream job, but it was like any other new business venture—very hard work for little or no money.

Sarah had let me know she was finished with the tour business and was developing a line of gluten-free hand cream products. It made sense, and I understood her wanting to pursue other endeavors. Italy had been my dream, first as a place to live, and now as a business. She had assisted in getting the second part of that dream off the ground, and I was grateful. I needed to figure out if it made economic sense for me to continue to run Tuscany tours for women.

My mind drifted to a conversation I had had with one of the widows on the last tour. She'd told me that despite making all of her trip payments, she hadn't been certain she could get on the plane and come to Italy. Her loss was still so new, and she'd never traveled without her husband.

As we leaned out of two windows on the top floor of Villa Marsili, overlooking the verdant valley below, she told me I was smart to *end* the tour in Cortona and not start it there. "If I'd seen this place first," she said, "I'd have never left!"

We had laughed and chatted like two Italian grandmas, hanging outside the screenless windows bordered by bright green shutters. And then she had added, "I want you to know, I've made a decision in the past few days."

"What's that?" I had asked her.

"I've decided I'm going to keep on living," she replied.

My eyes filled with tears, and I looked at her softly. She had tears in her eyes as well. I knew exactly what she meant. She was talking about the kind of living that included joy, and passion, and beauty.

We'd both been through some dark days, although our grief had been different. Days had passed for both of us that just included breathing but not really living. I hadn't shared the details of my grief with any of the ladies on the tour, and yet somehow they knew I understood.

I didn't want to let the concept of women's tours in Tuscany go. I loved the idea, and I had seen the magic that was created when women came together to celebrate a vacation in a gorgeous region. I needed to figure out how to continue the company and make a living in doing so.

I decided to take a walk by the Arno River, where I had walked so often in the past three years, ruminating on so many different things. The crowds began to increase each week since Easter, and I zigzagged through the back streets to avoid them. I crossed Ponte alle Grazie to the Oltrarno side and headed east toward Ponte di San Niccolò to a much quieter part of the city.

I talked to my angels as the late afternoon sun began to set. I told them, as if somehow these all-knowing beings knew nothing, that I had to make a living. I explained the dire facts, that the money I'd made from my house was dwindling away, and I was not getting any younger. I concluded with the fact that I knew the tours were making a difference in women's lives. I had seen it with each group, with each woman.

I crossed Ponte San Niccolò and turned west to head back toward the city. The sun was now behind Ponte Vecchio, and streaks of orange and pink blazed across the sky. I stopped to watch the sky and the river and leaned against the cement wall. *Aperitivo* hour was beginning, and the city was full of life and motion, but I stood alone with my favorite view.

I sighed deeply as I thought about how much I loved this city, this life, the time I had spent here, and the growth I had done. As I watched the fiery sun set, something caught my eye drifting out of the sky. I watched it come closer and then held out my hand. A white feather landed on the tip of my index finger, and I gazed at it in astonishment.

"I guess that's my answer," I said to the angels around me. I would have to trust that there was a way, and trust that I would figure it out. They hadn't let me down so far.

Seventy

With just a month left in Florence before I was to return to Utah for the summer, I wanted to savor each day. There would be time to put pencil to paper and figure out the financial reality of continuing a tour business here, but for now I had finished the accounting for the two spring tours and wanted to breathe in my city.

Relaxation and rejuvenation came in the form of walking in Florence, totally without a destination, without a schedule. I met friends for lunches and *aperitivo*, took one last trip to Cortona for the season, went to Impruneta to spend a day with Donatella and Andrea, and continued to contemplate what the next best step was for me.

I knew that turning Sarah's and my tour company into my own business would be a big undertaking, but it didn't scare me. I would need a new website, an assistant or two, a name for the business, a plan of action—but none of that felt overwhelming. I had learned, these past three years, I could always trust the process. The answer was waiting just below the surface, until I could be still enough to hear it.

Perhaps my strength had come from navigating through the Italian red tape, indifferent neighbors, or my biggest personal fear—being alone. Whatever the ultimate refining experience had been, the work had been done. I had come to know an inner strength and confidence that perhaps would have come anyway with age but surely came to me in these years, as *un regalo*—a gift from Italy.

Frequently, both at times I was frightened and times I felt strong, the words from "A Course in Miracles" would float through my mind. *If you knew who walked beside you at all times, on the path that you have chosen, you could never experience fear or doubt again.*

I began the too-familiar job of packing my suitcase for a summer in Utah. I would return to my apartment in Borgo Pinti mid-August, but Lorenzo would rent it out in the meantime. This generous arrangement meant I wouldn't pay for an empty apartment in Florence, and he would also store a suitcase here for me.

I picked up my favorite black boots and turned them over. I had worn all the way through the sole on one boot! They were beyond repair at this point, and so I tossed my fifth pair of Trooper boots in the garbage and ordered another pair online to be delivered to me in Salt Lake City. I could walk further in those boots than any I'd ever found, and I prayed they'd never be discontinued!

I had lived simply these past few years and let go of possessions with ease. Nothing I owned felt as precious to me as my memories, my experiences. I had time in the past week to sort through business cards and pictures from the last two tours and fully savor the explosion of recollections that they produced. I had done a few radio and magazine interviews and chuckled as, invariably, someone would use the phrase, "living the dream," in relation to my life.

I had let go of so much, both physically and mentally and, in that, I *had* found my dream, but I wasn't sure it would be anyone else's! On one of the last days in Florence that May, I stuffed my journal into my oversized leather purse and trekked across town to the Bardini Garden.

I entered off of via San Niccolò, my old street, into the cool green shade of my favorite garden. The steep climb up toward the small outdoor coffee bar took me through the wisteria-covered arch, and the intense bouquet permeated the air. I stopped to take in the panoramic view of Florence from Santa Croce to the Duomo to the Medici Chapels and Palazzo Vecchio.

The sun beat down as I sought refuge in the shade of the bar. Next month, I would let go of another decade—my fifties—and with June, turn sixty years old. It hadn't been an easy decade, without a doubt—the most difficult of my life. I pulled out my journal and began to make a list of all that I had released in order to sit in *this* spot, with *this* view, living *my* dream.

Here was my top ten:

1. **I let go of lengthy explanations.** "I'm sorry," sincerely said, is powerful. I've learned to give and receive a succinct apology. There's really nothing more that can be said.

2. **I let go of numbers.** I have purposefully not learned to convert my bathroom scale in Italy from kilos to pounds. I walk miles every day, eat fresh food, and my clothes fit. I'm not interested in the outside assessments that used to regulate my self-worth.

3. **I let go of looking for happiness.** When I finally embraced that a new relationship, place, or possession would not supply lasting happiness, I turned inward. It was then I realized it was up to me and always had been.

4. **I let go of judgment.** Living in a foreign country has convinced me that we each see through the lens of our own conditioning and culture. Every story is real to the person telling it. This much I know: life is long (if we are lucky), and karma's a bitch if we're jerks.

5. **I let go of fear.** If I can survive repeated visits to the Italian Questura, not much scares me. I know most of what I fear is out of my control, so I don't obsess over the details. Joy arrives when fear exits.

6. **I let go of possessions.** In traveling with two suitcases, I only hold on to the essentials and what I truly love. Memories are my souvenirs, and I am free from anything owning me.

7. **I let go of the past.** I have been many different people through the decades I have lived. I can't regret not having the wisdom at thirty that I have now at almost sixty. I did the best I could at the time, and I'm sure the people in my past did the same.

8. **I let go of noise.** There is a peace and wisdom found in silence that is often drowned out in daily life. It's become my place of sanity, and I love silence as much as I love music.

9. **I let go of being offended.** To be offended is to say that there is just one way to do something or one way to view it. I realize that to take offense is to offer a counter-attack, and I am not interested in doing that.

10. **I let go of the future.** Judging from my past, the future isn't going to run in a direct line, according to my best-laid plans. I loosely hold on to the reins and know I'll enjoy the adventure!

Seventy-one

Just as the sun was breaking in Florence, I looked out the airplane window to say a silent goodbye to my city. I would return in about two months, but I continued to watch until it disappeared from view. The short flight that morning was to Paris, and then the long flight to follow would be to Salt Lake City.

I had always chosen the same seat on my flights across the ocean between Paris and Salt Lake City, and my trip to Salt Lake City at the end of May 2015 was no different. What was different, however, was when I arrived at my seat, a child and her parents were waiting for me.

The dad, obviously American, launched into a long dialogue about me needing to change seats with him, and before I had a chance to answer, his asking had turned to demanding.

I asked where his seat was located, and when he pointed to a seat in the middle section, I shook my head, no, and indicated I wasn't interested in trading my front-row window seat for his. His face became red and his voice louder as he insisted I was to take his seat or face a trip across the ocean seated next to a child. I chuckled. I just don't meet that kind of drama with equal amounts of drama.

I turned back to the first-class cabin to ask a flight attendant for assistance. It took several minutes until an attendant was available to help us, and as I stood in the aisle, angry red-faced man gave her the details. When she turned to me to ask if I wanted to sit in his seat, I said, "No."

She left to see what other options were available, and I gazed around at the cabin full of travelers. I entertained myself with my usual game where in my mind I decided where each person was from, and where they were going. International travelers are a tired-looking group, and the dressed-for-comfort Americans were easy to peg. I had been up since four o'clock so I soon grew weary of my own game, leaned my heavy head against the partition behind me and tuned out the surrounding mini-dramas of my fellow passengers.

The flight was scheduled to depart in just a matter of minutes when the harried attendant returned and said my upgrade had been approved. That's flight attendant talk for I was moving on up—to first class!

I tried not to give a sucks-to-be-you look to the man who now had my original seat, breathed a sigh of relief that I wasn't married to him, and walked up to 6A, in the land of fully reclining seats.

I had been so tired all morning while traveling, but now I didn't feel like going to sleep. I leaned back and lifted the leg support part of my seat, so I now had the equivalent of a La-Z-Boy recliner in the sky. I gazed out the window at the expanse of blue, dotted by white puffs of clouds. I always imagined the clouds were filled with mini-trampolines that the angels bounced on for fun.

I drifted along with the hum of the airplane and the sweet space between fully awake and asleep. I thought about the past few days, saying goodbye to Donatella, and how sad she had looked when she told me, as she always did, that she worried I wouldn't return to Florence. No matter how I assured her I would, she would shake her head and tell me, "No, *cara*, one day you will go home and stay."

I thought about the flight from Salt Lake City to Florence in 2012, when I had panicked mid-flight that there may not really be a man named Lorenzo who had an apartment waiting for me. I remembered how apprehensive I felt to arrive in the city without knowing a single person or a single word of Italian. I had dared not give in to the torrential emotion that was welling up inside of me, and so I pushed it down so I could move forward.

I remembered making the trip after John and Thomas had teamed up together to exact their revenge, and how I had pulled out my passport and rubbed my fingers on the page with my attached visa for comfort. I'd not known on that flight what was to happen to me financially, but I had trusted in Greg to handle the legal details and in my angels, *and time,* to heal me.

I had made this flight across the Atlantic Ocean so many times, and on this day I looked at the vast sky with rays of light slicing through the clouds and felt nothing but peace. I knew there was work ahead, a lot of it, to get a young business off the ground. I knew there would be the constant job of trying to get the word out about the Tuscan tours for women, the endless hours of writing, posting, and advertising.

But I also knew that somewhere out in time and space, there was a group of women waiting to form who would see the dates and itinerary and find themselves in Tuscany. I had seen it happen enough times before to trust it would happen again. And I would be there to meet them, outside the revolving glass doors of Hotel Pierre, to welcome their jet-lagged selves to Florence and to an adventure of a lifetime! That was something I knew for sure.

I closed my eyes and reclined to horizontal. Burying under the down comforter and adjusting my pillow, I decided first class was nice—really nice. I was willing to work hard, put in the time, do whatever it took to run a business, write a book, or both, but I wanted to travel through the sky, and through life, on a first-class adventure!

Seventy-two

June 27, 2015

> *The circles of women around us weave invisible nets of love that carry us when we are weak and sing with us when we are strong.*
>
> —SARK

I realized as I looked out at the diverse group of women that I was the only one who recognized every face in the crowd. Jean had opened her home, nestled in the aspens against the rugged mountainside of Mount Olympus, for my birthday party.

In the group, spread out through the kitchen and great room, women from every decade of my life were meeting each other. It felt like a swirl of color and light—a net of laughter and love. Sixty years old didn't seem possible, but I was grateful to have had each and every year.

Shauna had flown in from Albuquerque, Sherrilee from California, and Lelan from Texas. I was thrilled that they had made such an effort to join with me for this milestone event. Lisa Jerome had brought a Chantilly and berry cake that was large enough to feed the entire neighborhood, and food and wine flowed. Lelan had purchased selfie sticks, which were the bane of my existence in Florence but the source of uncontrolled laughter and entertainment on this night!

Jean and I stepped outside on the balcony, which ran the length of the house and overlooked the valley. Setting low over the Great Salt Lake were the fiery colors of the Western sky—oranges, pinks, lavender, and purple hues. To the southwest were the Oquirrh Mountains, and behind me, the Wasatch Range. I had run from this city and these mountains, at one time. I had cursed the pain they seemed to hold for me, and I had wondered if I'd ever return, if I would ever want to.

But tonight the familiar purple outline of the mountains brought me comfort. I had been born and raised in this valley, fifth generation from the pioneers who walked with handcarts through those canyons. I knew its oddities and its beauty, but most of all, I knew it felt like home.

"Can you feel how many people love you, Lisa?" Jean asked me, as the sun slipped behind the lake.

From inside I could hear the voices and ripples of laughter from people I loved, and who had loved me, even in my absence. These were the women who had stood by me from elementary to high school drill team, to college, marriage, children, joys, and sorrows. They had each entered my life, and ultimately my soul, in different decades throughout my sixty years. They stayed connected to me, to share my story, even when my story happened half a world away.

I allowed myself to soak in all of their love that night as we retold stories, laughed, and cried over our memories together. I no longer was afraid to fully feel, fully experience, or express the divine gift of love. This was my tribe, this was loyalty, this was home; the hurt was gone, and I had healed.

I became aware that my words had conveyed the feeling in my heart long before my head caught on. When I was in Florence, I said I was going home in two weeks and meant Utah. When in Utah, going home meant back to Florence. And so it was. Both places felt like home to me now, and my heart was big enough to allow the duality, embrace the differences, and treasure the similarities.

I still felt a lump in my throat when I left either country, but not in a desperate sort of ripping away, as though I may never see it again. I knew now I would always return to each place, as long as I lived.

As Jean and I turned to walk back inside, I looked up to Mount Olympus, still green from the spring rain.

"Thank you," I whispered to the angels who walked beside me. Tomorrow I would be sixty, and I had never been happier.

Seventy-three

> *There are moments in our lives when we summon the courage to make choices that go against reason, against common sense and the wise counsel of people we trust. But we lean forward nonetheless because, despite all risks and rational argument, we believe that the path we are choosing is the right and best thing to do. We refuse to be bystanders, even if we do not know exactly where our actions will lead.*
>
> —Howard Schultz

I leaned forward in a tiny coffee shop in Rome in June 2012, just outside Armonia All'Opera B&B and across from the opera house, as I made an early-morning decision to find my joy. I leaned into a country that I knew nothing about, and it gently held me up with its ancient arms until I found my own strength. I leaned into the kindness of a culture and people completely foreign to me, and they softly accepted me into their hearts and taught me lessons I needed to know.

Sometimes Florence gave me tough love and sometimes pure grace, but she never let me fall. I have walked endless miles along the banks of the Arno River, to listen to the centuries-old songs of life in Tuscany and to the whisperings of my own heart. I have marveled at the surprises, the serendipity, and the sweetness of life that awaited me, at this point in my life, for taking such a leap of faith.

I leaned into the pain of my life, at times the darkest shadows of my heart, until I figured out how to let it all go. I leaned into my own shortcomings, the failings I tenaciously defended until I could make peace with them. It has taken these three years of waking up under the Tuscan sky, walking its cobblestone streets and my own raw vulnerability, to acknowledge, forgive, and make peace with it all. But I have done so.

In Italy, I'd stared down loneliness and long nights, but I'd also tasted newly pressed olive oil, Chianti wine, and Donatella's lasagna. I'd knelt where Saint Francis had prayed and sat with Michelangelo's *David* for entire afternoons. I'd been so alone, but also on the receiving end of immense kindness of strangers. I had lived fully, the highs and the lows, beyond my wildest dreams!

I had purposefully created my life exactly as I wanted it and decided not to hang around on the sidelines waiting for approval, direction, or security from anyone else. Finally! I had sought to jump into an adventure and was willing to pay the price for and accept the gifts it had to offer. With more years behind me than ahead, I was finished with timidity and uncertainty. Oh, how I have relished my years in Italy!

I leaned forward now to create a new company that reflected my philosophy on travel, Tuscany, and women coming together. *Find Yourself in Tuscany* was the perfect name for what I wished to convey. I wanted to be the catalyst to provide women an opportunity to find their own joy and experience Tuscany as a local!

In the early-morning hours of my sixtieth birthday, I left my party and stumbled to bed content and happy. The summer sky was clear in Salt Lake City, and the stars served as twinkling night lights outside my bedroom window.

I closed my eyes and felt my body sink into the futon that serves as my bed here. On that night, as I often did in my last wakeful minutes, I flew my soul to Florence. High on the hill

I perched atop San Miniato and looked at the view of terracotta roofs and five bridges. I heard the bells peal their familiar cadence from the campanile, and I could see my beloved city with her white, green, and rose marble churches against the azure sky. The turquoise dome of the synagogue in Borgo Pinti and rust-colored domes of the Medici Chapels and the Duomo served as my compass, and in my mind, I traversed the street to see the top of my apartment building on via di Mezzo. In my dreaming now, I turned my gaze to the south to take in the olive groves spotted with peach and ocher-colored stucco estates, and I breathed in the last of the season's wisteria. *Ritornerò, amore*, I promised as I drifted off...I will always return to you.

> *We shall not cease from exploration, and the end of all our exploring will be to arrive where we started and know the place for the first time.*
>
> —T. S. Eliot

Epilogue

You can't connect the dots looking forward; you can only connect them looking back. So you have to trust that the dots will somehow connect in your future.
—Steve Jobs

As I finish the last edits of this book, I am beginning my fifth year in Florence. Since my sixtieth birthday, the last chapter of *I Found Myself in Tuscany*, I have led five more groups of women through Tuscany, hired my daughter as my assistant, and have tours booked through October 2017.

During the fourth year in Italy, situations arose that had me in the U.S. for a longer period of time than I had planned. With that shift, I found another rhythm to dance to—half of the time in Florence, half in Salt Lake City. It was unplanned but aligned perfectly with my soul's desire for that year.

I continue to struggle and to appreciate the muddy middle of life—the part where I am unsure. The beginning of each thread, whether a grand undertaking or a small step, is easily defined—the jumping-off point. The ending, when it arrives with its measured results, is fairly easily defined as well. It's in the middle—murky and seemingly directionless—where trust has to take the wheel. When it's impossible to see the finish line, the payoff, reason, or success, what is it that propels us to continue to move forward? The murky, muddy middle has become my greatest teacher. I am trying to lean into the uncertainty and enjoy that part of the journey as I continue to chase my dreams.

In the moments when I can't see my way through, I think about the chapters of my love story with Italy. I remember long walks along the Arno River where I begged my angels for an answer to why I was there, and I remember the shimmering palm trees in the moonlight over Bardini Garden on those sleepless nights when loneliness and fear won out. I recall moments of serendipity and joy as people arrived in my life and doors opened to me, a new business was created, and the grace with which it all unfolded. Italy took me home because home is in my heart, and I carry that wherever I go.

Acknowledgments

When I left for Florence, Italy, I thought I was going alone. I was unaware that the friendships of my lifetime would make the journey with me. I was equally unaware of the friends on the other side of the ocean who were awaiting my arrival. For all the love and kindness I've received along the way, I am forever grateful.

Special thanks to the groups of women I've shared decades of friendship with, for your support then and now—the Skyline girls, my Alpha Chi Omega sisters, my fitness students, and my first and forever friend, Gayle Platt Spjut.

I have such gratitude for Linda Secrist for encouraging me to write a book four years before I did so, and Susie Martindale, Lisa Jerome, and Jennifer Baguley for endless support. To the Dodo girls (Sherrilee Seibert, Jane Rogers, Lelan Daines, and Jean Mack), Shauna Offret, Vikki Carrel, Carolyn Roll—you are as close as sisters, and I thank you for a lifetime of walking beside me. For my brother, Vance, one of the finest people I've ever known, thank you, and to my parents, my gratitude for sharing the importance of travel.

Thank you, Jolene Green, for providing clarity and compassion. Connie Weissinger Tucker and Caroline Larsen, thank you for your editing and guidance through this process.

Lorenzo Clemente, Andrea Vignoli, Donatella Zolfanelli, Alexandra Lawrence—you are my Italian family, and I will hold you in my heart forever as that.

Caitlin Swanson, Elizabeth Orchard, Georgette Jupe Pradier, and Nardia Plumridge, thank you for creating quick, strong bonds of friendship. The expat community in Florence was a source of immediate strength and inclusion, and I appreciate the women from the U.S. and the U.K. with whom I shared countless hours. I have treasured my time in our tight-knit club!

In deepest gratitude, I thank my angels from the other side, whom I felt beside me so often in Italy, and while writing my story—especially Amy Stewart, Bonnie Calder, Kim Duffin, Richard Barnum-Reese—you live forever in my heart.

And most of all, thank you to my children, Justin Wood and Lauren Wood. I gave you your wings, and then you gave me mine. I love you to the moon and back.

44672118R00174

Made in the USA
San Bernardino, CA
20 January 2017